WHAT PEOPLE ARE SAYING ABOUT

ETERNAL WAY TO BLISS

"I am happy you wrote a book on Hinduism. Love and Blessings."
Sri Sri Ravi Shankar. Renowned spiritual leader. Founder, Art of Living Foundation

"Congratulations to Vinita on her hard work to produce this book which covers some concepts of Hinduism. May this work become her worship to God and may it lead her to further spiritual journey. Best wishes."
Br. Prabodh Chaitanya, Chinmaya Mission San Jose, CA

"This book is a welcome addition to the literature that brings the wisdom of the Vedic seers to life for modern seekers. As a Hindu of Indian descent living in America, and as a householder with a family and a career in Silicon Valley, Vinita Pande brings a much-needed perspective to the practical application of ancient teachings to the demands of today's world. Nothing is more important than the integration of East and West, and this book can help advance that ongoing process."
Philip Goldberg, author of "American Veda: From Emerson and the Beatles to Yoga and Meditation, How Indian Spirituality Changed the West"

"Vinita Pande's excellent book is highly readable and most enjoyable, to say the very least. It tells the story of an exhaustive spiritual search through the experiences of an ordinary girl named Kesari. The book is in fact the culmination of the Author, Vinita Pande's, long and extensive practical study into all [ ]
with particular emphasis on the E
Guru is the famed Sri Sri Ravi Sh

dedicated application and Yoga practice, she has arrived at the gateway to Liberation, under the ultimate guidance of Sat Guru Sri Bhagavan Ramana Maharshi. I heartily recommend this book to all interested in Non Dualism and those wishing to discover a practical and infallible way to Self Realisation."
Alan Jacobs, Poet Writer Author, President, Ramana Maharshi Foundation UK

Vinita Pande's Eternal Way to Bliss documents her explorations into the ancient Hindu path of bhakti (love of the Divine), the lessons she has learned and her experiences, musings, feelings and personal growth along the way. Starting from her distress and disillusionment with the world and other human beings, this Krishna devotee articulates her search for answers, meaning and essential Consciousness and Bliss, primarily through the teachings of the Bhagavad Gita and of her guru, Sri Sri Ravi Shankar. Her acknowledgment of selfless service as a necessary prelude to meditation—so frequently overlooked in this day and age—is most welcome. "I have seen people talk the highest knowledge and not live the basics," she shares. "What's the point? It's useless. Better to live the basics and let the highest knowledge dawn naturally, like the ripening of a fruit."
Sadasivanatha Palaniswami, Editor-in-Chief, Hinduism Today magazine.

"Vinita Pande has a clear understanding of the steps and stages on the spiritual path. With insight and compassion she guides the reader on the journey to the Self."
Swami Prasannatmananda, Vedanta Society, Berkeley, CA

Eternal Way to Bliss

Kesari's Quest for Answers,
Solutions and Meaning

Eternal Way to Bliss

Kesari's Quest for Answers, Solutions and Meaning

Vinita Dubey Pande

MANTRA
BOOKS

Winchester, UK
Washington, USA

First published by Mantra Books, 2013
Mantra Books is an imprint of John Hunt Publishing Ltd., Laurel House, Station Approach,
Alresford, Hants, SO24 9JH, UK
office1@jhpbooks.net
www.johnhuntpublishing.com
www.mantra-books.net

For distributor details and how to order please visit the 'Ordering' section on our website.

Text copyright: Vinita Dubey Pande 2013

ISBN: 978 1 78099 859 6

Design: Stuart Davies

Printed in the USA by Edwards Brothers Malloy

We operate a distinctive and ethical publishing philosophy in all
areas of our business, from our global network of authors to
production and worldwide distribution.

CONTENTS

Om Swastih[1]

With deepest reverence and gratitude I offer this at the feet of Sri Krishna, my mother, my late father, my Gurudev, and all enlightened masters.

---

1 *Om* – sound vibration for cosmic consciousness. *Swastih* – auspiciousness, prosperity, well, being, blessings.

ACKNOWLEDGMENTS

I am thankful to my two sons for giving me feedback, support, and doing the initial edits on my manuscript. I am deeply grateful to my mother for her unconditional love and blessings. I value the honest feedback from my husband, Atul Pande, because he usually mirrors public opinion. I would like to thank my sister-in-law, Nargess Dubey, for her kindness in reading the first draft of some chapters. Many thanks to my most dynamic sister-in-law, Sangeeta Pande, and my talented best friend, Tanuja Pande, for their artistic inputs. I would also like to thank my niece, Noopur Tiwari, for her support. Kunal Mukherjee, a published author and a dear friend, has been very kind in helping and guiding me. So thankful to all my friends including; Madhu Dhillon, Punit Mahendru, Ramnee alumni, Art of Living peers, and friends on Facebook for reading my book blog, and for their encouragement.

A PERSONAL INTRODUCTION

My knowledge is not yet complete - only a realized one's is. If I waited until I became perfect before I wrote, I would never write. This knowledge is not mine; these pages present my reflections on the eternal knowledge that was revealed to ancient sages around the globe. Knowledge is inherent in cosmic consciousness, and therefore has no beginning and not of human origin. Cosmic consciousness is pure existence, eternal knowledge, and infinite: *Satyam Jnanam Anantam Brahman.* Much later it was codified into the four Vedas. The knowledge in the Vedas, the Brahma Sutras and the Bhagavad Gita is considered "complete."

With God's grace I have had the interest in seeking truth and knowledge. I am deeply grateful to my Guru, Sri Sri Ravi Shankar for his love and grace. He has given me so much knowledge; techniques such as pranayama, yoga, meditation; and most of all, the experience of my true nature. The world has been blessed with many masters over the ages who have brought this eternal knowledge to the world. I am also grateful to the Chinmaya Mission for being the flag bearers of Vedanta. These are some of the wonderful works of great masters that I have been fortunate enough to read and listen to:

Tattva Bodha. Atma Bodha. Narad Bhakti Sutra. Patanjali Yoga Sutras. Isha Upanishad. Kena Upanishad. Katho Upanishad. Chhandogya Upanishad. Kaivalya Upanishad. Bhagavad Gita. Ashtavakra Gita. Yoga Vasistha. Kapila Gita. Sadacarah. Aparoksanubhuti. Mahabharat. Ramayan. I have studied the teachings of Vivekananda, Ramana Maharishi, Sri Sri Ravi Shankar, and others. I've also studied Ayurveda, the practice of Yoga and meditation, and have accessed several other knowledge sources.

I

This list is just a small fraction of the knowledge under the umbrella of Vedic texts. I would like to learn all four Vedas. However, as Ramana Maharishi said, it's not about numbers: you only need one mirror to see your true reflection.

There are so many people who have greater knowledge than I, who are more realized than I, who can write better than I. There are three types of understanding; intellectual, experiential and existential realization (when it becomes your very nature). This writing is about my present understanding of this knowledge, expressed from an experiential standpoint.

In addition to my reflections, I have taken great care in verifying the knowledge that I present here, often referring to the source, and also can be verified, so I would like the reader to rest assured that the information here is reliable. However, even in the Vedic tradition there are different commentaries, I have used the known authorities in the subject. I have definitely not put in all that is included in Vedic wisdom. Volumes have been written for thousands of years on this wisdom. What I have presented is the core theme.

This book follows the same core theme as the Bhagavad Gita:

Chapter 1: Like the Bhagavad Gita, Yoga Vasistha, and as in the story of Buddha, the journey starts from grief, with a deep questioning.

Chapter 2: The second chapter pretty much summarizes the whole book.

Chapter 3: "Karma Yoga," or the wisdom on how to act, is the topic of the third chapter.

Chapter 4: The fourth chapter is on meditation or Upasana.

Chapter 5: One of my favorite chapters is on devotion.

Chapter 6 and 7: These do not have corresponding chapters in the Gita but I have written as preparation for knowledge of the Self.

Chapter 8 and 9: These chapters are on the knowledge of the Self, Jnan Yoga.

Chapter 10: Describes the enlightened one.

Chapter 11: A summary of the book in personal terms, with love, for my son.

Those who are familiar with Vedic teachings may find hidden themes and implied meanings.

I have read many modern, western, New Age, and scientific presentations of Vedic knowledge. I have deliberately made the tone of this book more authentic because I didn't want to dilute or deviate from how the masters of Vedanta expound this knowledge. Therefore, I have used the original method and approach used in Vedic texts such as the Bhagavad Gita. I am a modern woman in the technology field and I have a family. I have lived in many places around the world. I have found that I gained the most from a traditional approach to this wisdom, and I believe a lot of people around the world will be able to relate to it as well.

The terms "Hindu" and "Hinduism" are not indigenous to India; neither is the name "India"! The river Sindhu in Bharat (India) was called "Hindus" by the Persians and later "Indus" by the Greeks, and was also a term for the people who live east of this river. The names "India," "Hindu," and "Hinduism" come from these. If there is a native name for this ancient wisdom tradition it is "Sanatana Dharma," the universal eternal laws of nature. However, it is often referred to simply as Shastras amongst practitioners and in the texts which literally means science. I will use the term "Vedic" in the book.

With that said, let's enter the projection of my mind, the expression of my heart and the essence of my soul.

1 VENTING

After four decades on the planet it is very clear to me that I don't want to be here. Sad but true. Everything and everyone I see here, I think, is at least 80 percent negative, including me. In this pathetic state of affairs I need to survive.

I am disappointed with everyone's immoral character - their complex egos, the games they play, their nastiness; the list can be endless. Some are simply demons, and I've written them off. I mean, just look at the people in this world; in any group of ten people, eight of them will have 80 percent negative qualities. It is hard to find good values in people. The same is true for me! I am disappointed in myself; I am just a crumb on this earth. I am nowhere I aspire to be. I can't deal with people (as you can see); I am short-tempered, impatient, controlling, and more. I don't know anything. I talk too much. I am sure others have the same opinion of me that I have of them.

I am disgusted with the worst of people dominating and driving things, while the silent minority, who are good, refrain from expressing themselves and hide in a corner. Everywhere I look, whether it's the work environment or social groups, wherever there are people, negativity dominates. My spiritual master tells me that negativity is on the surface and the core is positive, like in an atom. Well, it's the negativity we have to deal with - how often do we meet someone whose purity and perfection shines through?

Negativity is so difficult to get rid of. Past events leave an impression on my mind; if something bad happens today, I will be sulking tomorrow too. If only I could have no negative impressions about people or events, have no negative emotions poisoning my system, what a great benefit it would be. If I woke up each morning and started afresh with no negativity, no taints on my heart or mind, it would be such a relief.

The world has become a display of ego, greed, selfishness, anger, hatred, and utter ignorance. We have developed so much materially, but I feel as human beings we are degenerating. Are the standards for friendship and humanity falling with passage of time? Are we at the lowest point in humanity, and is this world close to becoming a living hell? Or is it going to get worse still?

Look at politicians. Recently I dived deep into Indian politics and came to the conclusion that it's so bad, nothing can be done; it's simply headed toward the edge of a steep cliff. It's because the power is in the wrong hands, the worst people are running the show, too many people are immoral, and the system doesn't work. The bad people are united and the good people are divided.

I really see no reason to live. Maybe I should just go and live in some small village, where people are simple, innocent, and still have some values. At least I'll live the rest of my life peacefully - since I have to go through life anyway. The only people I truly love are my mother, my father, and my two sons, and I find them the only reason for living.

Spiritual teachers say life's purpose is self-realization, enlight-enment. So what exactly is that? Yes, we have all heard it, and we just have to have faith in scriptures that it exists. But when someone attains enlightenment, what happens? Something happens to them inside, but what? A no-mind state perhaps. What exactly is that: no-mind, no ego? I've heard that enlightened people merge with cosmic consciousness. Okay, that's just too far out for me; I don't understand – or do they still human or they become ETs? Scary. Is it some psycho state? Do I really want enlightenment?

I think I was quite happy as an innocent little girl, not knowing anything. I was just happy being me, simple and natural, with no care in the world, for my little world was perfect. Isn't that Nirvana? But then it had to change. I had to grow up, become miserable, and then struggle to seek freedom from that misery. Now I'm stuck. No way out, not knowing where to go - what is the way forward? Even when I die, I will just come back here again to be miserable.

What's the purpose of living? I can't simply turn a blind eye to these questions and live like a robot, or have this herd mentality: everyone is simply living and so should I. I can't follow the patterns everyone else is: go to school, find a job, get married, have kids, work some more, retire, and then finally die. All this for what? Most people don't even ask this question. They simply live their lives like cattle in a herd and follow the norms of the world and do what everyone else is doing.

Don't people ever wonder what they are living for? The biggest wake-up call is death. But by then it's too late to aim for self-realization. If, having seen someone die, one doesn't start living, he or she has missed the opportunity of a lifetime. There are so many depressed people and so much sickness and suffering. Is it just me, or are most people unhappy? Are people only feigning happiness? That superficial happiness evaporates very quickly when faced with a problem, to be replaced with sadness or anger. Most people go through this yo-yo of happiness and sadness all their lives, never attaining equilibrium.

I am confused, and I really feel like I am at rock bottom in my life, trying to find some meaning to it. Tired of the mundane, going through the motions of life day, in and day out.

7

I have read so much, heard so much, and done so much, but still I am nowhere. I am supposed to be spiritual - because I need it the most I think. Look at me. I am a total failure! I still have the same problems, still crying about this and that.

The whole world has dried up around me. The only oasis is the lectures I attend given by Swami-ji[2] at the local monastery. In the Bhagavad Gita class today, we learned that there *will* be misery, sickness, death, and other problems. It is the nature of the world. It is the nature of the body and mind. While the *mind* is going through this duality of happiness/sadness, anger/attraction, we need to remain aware of our Eternal Self, which is untouched. And while the *body* may be going through the opposites of health/sickness, youth/aging, we need to be aware that we are not the body but the Eternal Self, that is untouched. Hmmm...It sounds good but hard to practice. Although I must admit that when I was sick yesterday and landed in the ER, I could observe the body and say, "The body is going through something" and I observed the body to see what was going on inside. So I have made some progress. But a few days ago, someone at work gave me a lot of grief and I was truly thrown off my center, lost balance, and reacted.

Why do I react? Why do I get angry? Why am I defensive when blamed and criticized? What others do is their *Karma*; how I react is mine. I need to detach. I need to be more aware. I need to say "No!" I need to observe my urge to react and take a deep breath. I need to be smart to tackle difficult people for my own benefit. Otherwise, it is I who gets hurt. "Having resentment is like drinking poison and thinking that it'll kill your enemy," said Nelson Mandela. Others should not be able to control me, affect

---

2   Swami: Hindu monk. Literally means, established in the Self. "-ji" added for reverence like in Gandhi-ji.

my health, or disturb my mind.

I'm tired. Oh, Krishna, please help me! Where are you? You are my only hope.

> *"Giridhar Gopāl ne hi pyār nibhāyā, kisi dosare ne nāhi.*
> *Baki sab kā pyār badalā, mere Giridhar kā kabhi nāhi.*
> *Mere to Giridhar Gopal dosaro na koi."*
> *"Vohi mera sāth nibhāte, vohi meri rakshā karte.*
> *Vohi mere Priya! Mere Paramatmā! Mero pati soi."*

Translation:

> *Only Giridhar Gopal (Krishna) fulfilled his promise of love and no one else.*
> *Everyone else's love changed but never my Giridhar Gopal's.*
> *Only Giridhar Gopal is mine and no one else.*
> *Only He is my true companion, only He protects me.*
> *Only He is my beloved, my divine, my soul mate.*

On this darkest night of creation, where everything seems to have reached deep into the abyss of evolution, there is nothing but evil. The only option is total destruction for a fresh start. The only path is upward now. It has to be after reaching absolute bottom. Knowing that this, too, will change, knowing that this dark evil night is the climax of creation, I see a ray of hope. Without this knowing, I would be forever lost in misery. I, too, have reached the bottom, searching for a way up and out, searching for the Self. Without the desire to know "Who am I?" I would be forever stuck with the miserable "I." Still, I have a faint feeling that there is a better "I," a happier "I," that I have to get back to. When one's self-esteem is at the lowest a "knowing" has to awaken. So I tell myself, "Kesari, wake up!"

I tread the path in search of that pure self, that awakened self. I can fall no further into that inner pit. I have to find a way out. This, too, will change; this night will be over. There will be another day whose dawn will illumine the true me. I will smile again. Where art thou, Krishna, my savior? My love for you is like nectar in this dry dusty desert. It has helped me survive. Tell me now the way forward, come to my help. Offer me some hope and knowledge, show me the way. I trust you and only you. Krishna, please come to me! Krishna! Krishna! *Krishna*!

2 DAWN OF A NEW DAY

The darkest night is over. Coincidentally, it was '*Mahalaya Amavasya*,' or 'no moon night' symbolizing cosmic dissolution in an ancient eastern tradition. This is followed by the nine nights for cosmic creation, '*Navratri*'. In this ancient wisdom creation is considered cyclical not linear.

It's the dawn of a new day. I have decided to look at the world differently. When stuck in one perspective the opposite view is a savior. There can be a shift when you look at things in a different light. So let me explore a completely different way of looking at myself, my life, and this world.

It's all in the mind; I know this. My world is a projection of my mind. Whatever I project is reflected back to me.

I turn to wisdom to remove the darkness. I have faith in the ancient, time-tested knowledge of the Vedas and the Bhagavad Gita. It understands human beings, creation, and consciousness so well. It has led so many to liberation. Like the axis of the earth, we should be centered in its wisdom, and not deviate from it.

To understand them correctly I have been attending this lecture series by Swami-ji, who is an expert in these scriptures. He's a monk dedicating his life to the spiritual path. I went there early today to ask Swami-ji for some advice.

He was leaving from his room for the lecture hall and I caught him just in time. "Swamiji I have a question," I said. "Sometimes I find it just too difficult to go on. I mean there are so many serious problems and challenges in my life, I don't know how to face them, overcome them, or even if I have the will to go on. Is there some solution in our scriptures that will help me lead a productive, meaningful life?"

"Of course," he said with confidence. "See these problems

and challenges as part of a game, like a video game. Otherwise how will life be fun, and how will you end up winning in the end? Come, let's go to the lecture, you will find many answers." Still processing his reply, I followed him to the hall.

As soon as I entered the hall I melted into the calming presence of the environment. I found a seat and sat down. Everyone was silently waiting for the lecture to begin. Swamiji went up to the front, and sat down cross-legged on a small platform,dressed in orange robes, always a slight smile on his face, glowing. Radiant. His presence is so overwhelmingly peaceful and calm that all my gazillion thoughts and complaints come to rest. I'm ready to listen.

"Isha vasyam idam sarvam." Swamiji says the first verse of the Isha Upanishad. "See God, consciousness, pervading everything, as the substratum of everything. See this whole creation as a divine Being. This is the vision of truth," he explains. Adi Shankaracharya, a sage from India in the middle ages, also said that if you look at the world from a divine vision, you will see the whole world permeated by consciousness.

So it's up to me how I view the world. It is easy to see divinity in good people but not in evil people. However, evil people can also become good again, so they have to be inherently good as well. If everyone and everything is God, why did He create imperfection in the world?

Oh, wait: Everything in the world is imperfect by design!

There's a Sanskrit mantra, *"Purnam Adah Purnam Idam,"* which means "That (consciousness) is complete...whole, and This (world) is also complete and whole." Everything is exactly as it's meant to be, so why should I suffer? I suffer because I'm not in sync with this divine design.

I need to be in sync with both creation and consciousness, with the imperfect and the perfect. It is very important for me to realize the misery is from seeking perfection in people, situations, and myself but never finding it. My misery is also by design. Otherwise, how will I look for perfection inside? So I say to myself, "Relax. It's okay, everything is imperfect. That's the way it's meant to be."

Swamiji continues, "*Yat kinca jagatyaam Jagat.* The Sanskrit word *Jagat* describes this creation; it means that which comes and goes and stays only for a short while." Essentially, everything in the world is changing, nothing is permanent. Seeking permanence in anything: love, friendship, jobs, or money is futile. Everything and everyone will change; it's natural. Yet again and again I seek permanence. It changes and I sulk. I want to hold on, like trying to grasp the wind in my fist, or arrest the flow of a river, not wanting it to flow away.

So a change in vision is required to see life and the world in a different light. Swamiji says that the way to prepare for this shift, according to ancient sages, is to attain discriminating wisdom (*Vivek*); dispassion (*Vairagya*); the six wealths, including faith (*Shraddha*); and the yearning to be free (*Mumukshutva*).

When life is going good, when we're happy, we never think of being free, pray to God, ponder questions about life, or ask "Who am I?" There is no need. Very few seek liberation, Moksha, when happy. Sri Krishna says that there are three types of people who come looking for God:

1. Those who want to get rid of problems and misery.
2. Those who want to gain something: a job, wealth, health, a child, whatever the object of desire is.
3. Those who are sincere seekers of truth.

I have seen friends who become spiritual when they lose a job, or when they get health problems, or something bad happens to a family member. But a wise person who seeks the truth, God, and Self, even in happy times, will never become miserable in bad times. There is a saying on this by the fifteenth century Indian sage, Kabir:

"Dukh mein sumiran sab karen, sukh mein kare na koi. Jo sukh mein sumiran kare, to dukh kahe ko hoy."

This ancient Vedic wisdom understands life so well. I am fortunate that there's someone who has so much experience of this knowledge to explain it to me. Here's how Swamiji puts it:

Problem definition: There is misery in life from problems related to health, wealth, relationships, and children. What values define a "good human being," and how do we overcome the obstacles to becoming one?
Cause:

1. Ignorance.
2. A disturbed and restless mind.
3. Negativity or impurities like cravings (*raga*), aversions (*dwesh*), desires (*kama*), anger (*krodha*), greed (*lobha*), delusion (*moha*), self-infatuation (*mada*), jealousy (*matsarya)*, malice (*asuya*), envy (*irsya), *hypocrisy (*dambha),* pride (*darpa*), fear *(bhay),* and *ego* (*ahamkara*).

Solution: What is the solution? The solutions follow...

God, or nature, gave us this life with its challenges and also handed us a solutions manual to figure out how to be happy. It lists the values we should incorporate to be a good human being. One such guide is the Bhagavad Gita. It's perfect because it's complete; nothing is missing.

According to an eastern wisdom tradition there is a path of evolution for an individual soul (*Jiva*) from the time it's created, separated from cosmic consciousness, to the many lives it lives, then the final merging back into consciousness (enlightenment). That prescribed path for a successful life was explained by Swamiji as follows:

First: **Principles for Action (*Karma Yoga*).** Do your duties; fulfill your roles, work. This is external effort. *Karma Yoga* means serving others and dedicating this service to God. Serving without expecting anything in return, going beyond the ego, not being propelled by selfish desires, or being attached to the results. Another aspect of this wisdom for acting in the world is to know that you are not the doer, that everything is happening *through* you. It means at every step, having righteousness and the laws of nature (*Dharma*) illuminate your path.

What is *Dharma*? The universe was created with certain laws. Some of the physical laws that govern creation are contained in physics, chemistry and biology. Then there are laws that govern subtler aspects such as the mind. There are laws for plants, for the animal kingdom and for human life. When you are in rhythm with the laws of nature then you attain your natural self –that's pure existence, consciousness, love, bliss. When we live our life in harmony with these natural laws then naturally the following three manifest: material prosperity (*Artha*); fulfillment of desires (*Kama*); and enlightenment (*Moksha*).

Actions done in accordance with Dharma removes impurities from our minds and emotions, subdues the ego, and reduces desires. Selfless service benefits others, and indirectly, oneself also. Most of us are in this stage of evolution,yet so many jump to meditation or knowledge before this critical step of purification. It's like a cake recipe, you need to add the right ingredients and follow the directions.

Second: **Spiritual practices (*Upasana*)**. This is the internal letting go. It includes: Yoga, Pranayama, meditation, worship, and devotion. These practices are prescribed to calm the disturbed, restless mind and bring faith. They will settle the mind to the extent that impurities have been removed in the first step.

And finally **knowledge (*Jnan*)** to purify the intellect, lift the veil covering our true Self, remove ignorance by gaining Self-knowledge, and make consciousness an experiential reality. The values and virtues we need to live are also knowledge. If we have impurities and a disturbed mind knowledge will just be information not wisdom.

In short: If you have muddy and turbulent waters, how can you see the depth? So first we need to remove the mud, then we need to calm the surface, then we can see the depth and a clear reflection of our Self.

How do we integrate more and more of this knowledge? Swamiji says that spiritual masters have said that, for most people, it's a continuum of growth that occurs over lifetimes.

Our *Shastras* say that we need to keep practicing — listening to knowledge (*Shravanam*), reflecting (*Mananam*), and meditating to realize (*Nididhyasanam*) — over and over again.

The ripening of the fruit takes time, and when the fruit is ripe it will fall. We don't know when or how — it just happens. The fruit of our actions is not in our hands.

Events come and go. People come and go. The world keeps turning.

Nothing matters. Don't worry, be happy! Enjoy this moment. As I drive back home from the lecture on this beautiful moonlit night, alone, I put on my favorite Sufi song, singing, smiling, and swinging, the mystical meaning of the lyrics giving me goose bumps. Who cares about the rest of the world? This is my journey; let me celebrate my time here.

One day I, too, will go, and what happens after that? I don't know and can't know, so let it happen, flow with it, be with it. Peace!

Like Buddha said, sorrow, misery, sickness, and death are going to be there. They're a part of life. We shouldn't let them make us miserable. I have to get back in touch with that space in me that is peaceful and blissful, and separate myself from this misery. That space within me is never changing; there's a substratum that is changeless and permanent. Knowing this difference is called discriminating wisdom (*Vivek*) in the Vedic texts. I have lost touch with it, and therefore I am miserable. As soon as I get back in touch with my Self, I'm in bliss. When I am more established in myself, that centeredness brings calm. Being aware brings calm. And when I am calm, I make fewer mistakes in dealing with people and situations. Problems will still be there, but when I am established in my Self, I can surf the waves of problems and no longer get battered by them or drown.

Knowing this, I need to fully engage in the world and play by its far from perfect rules. If I hate them, I'll be unhappy. So while I participate in the imperfect world outside, I need to be detached (*Vairagya*) inside, otherwise I will again be miserable. In both the outer realm of imperfection and the inner realm of perfection, I need to be in harmony. Stress and misery come when I'm in disharmony with the rhythms of the universe. All the wheels of the clock need to move in harmony.

What am I looking for in this life? *I just want to be happy!* Not just now, but always, every moment. No matter what happens, it should not affect my happiness. I want happiness that's unlimited, permanent, and infinite. But everything gives me only momentary happiness. I get a new car and love it for a few days and after that it's like any other car. It's same thing with a new gadget, a new house, or any shiny distraction. Most people think that money will make them happy, yet many rich people can't even sleep well at night! Many look for job satisfaction: they live to work rather than work to earn a living. Then one day they lose their job. Those who want to get married think they will be happy once they find the perfect spouse; those who've been married for years envy single people! I have done everything to find this permanent happiness—in relationships, friendships, new jobs, homes, cities, and material things; taken vacations and spiritual courses, and waited for better times. Basically, I have looked for the perfect happiness externally, in places, things, people, and haven't found it.

The next day, as I take my evening walk I tell myself, "Okay, now I have to understand what Swamiji was talking about yesterday." There are two aspects to life: First is the "I" within who witnesses, feels, thinks, experiences; the second is that which is experienced or known, like the world, my body, breath, mind, and emotions. If happiness could be attained by acquiring things, then happiness would not change with time, place, or circum-stances. But it does. So if happiness isn't the nature of objects, it has to be inherent in the subject, the "I." There's no third aspect. Therefore "I" must be the source of happiness. Logical, right? So the seeking outside needs to change to seeking within. It makes sense. Happiness has to be my nature-that's why I seek it. When I'm removed from it I'm constantly trying to get back to it. And happiness feels natural. Not sorrow; it's not my nature so I want to get rid of it. Our true nature according to the ancient Vedic texts (Shastras), is Existence, Consciousness, Bliss (Sat Chit Anand).

My son said to me one day that reading the Bhagavad Gita feels good, but *implementation* is what's important and yet so difficult. Those who are spiritual and are learning from a guide need to see how much knowledge has integrated in us. How we handle people or a problem tests how much the knowledge has become living wisdom. How far back we fall and how low, or if we fall and recover quickly, or we don't fall at all, reveals how truly wise we have grown. The lesser the misery, the more the knowledge has been integrated.

All this theory is good but the most precious; the most beautiful thing in my life is **devotion**. No need to gain it, learn it, or make any effort—it's mine already. And no one can take that away from me. It is eternal, it is always with me. Who needs knowledge? Knowledgeable ones bow to the feet of a devotee— they thirst for a drop of the nectar of devotion. This ocean of divine love in my heart is the source of the all rivers of love. This is the mother of compassion. This *Russ* (nectar) and *Bhāv* (devotional ecstasy) dissolves me into eternal bliss.

Leave me, let me rejoice in this drunken state - I am intoxicated with boundless bliss. No meditation can match its sweetness; no knowledge can reach its grandeur. Love is supreme. It is me.

But then a wise voice within says, "No, no, all paths are supreme. Faith, devotion, knowledge are all one, expressed differently in each of us."

Now it's the eighth day of the nine nights of "*Navratri.*" Had a prayer at home and several ladies came. Feels so sacred and serene. The smell of camphor, incense, oil lamps, and flowers makes the atmosphere so divine. Later on this long rainy night I am alone, and all the lights are off. Just looking outside the window, in the lamp light I see the branches of the trees waving in the wind and rain,the pitter-patter on the rooftop like a lullaby. Let me close my eyes and be that child again...simple, natural, innocent, with the spark of divinity, purity, peace, and bliss…

I curl into the warm, comfortable lap of Mother Nature like a baby, and slip into sleep…

3 HOW TO BE A MILLIONARE

There was a lot of knowledge and information in the last lecture by Swamiji to integrate instantly. It's like being handed a concise comprehensive summary of an entire encyclopedia in a one hour lecture. I need to digest it bit by bit. Let me start with understanding the first step of spiritual evolution, the Yoga of Action or *Karma Yoga*.

I am Indian, and we tend to be very social people. Our get-togethers are very interesting because we don't feel shy about voicing our opinions, or giving advice. We are also very passionate and emotional people. We are NRIs (Non-Resident Indians) living in Silicon Valley, and guess what? We're all in IT.

So what do you think most of the conversations are about? Work, companies, technology, stocks, IPOs, H1, green cards, deals to buy...but because of my interest in spirituality, sometimes the conversations turn into philosophical discussions. My friends know how passionate Kesari (that's me) is about spirituality, and loves to preach her knowledge!

Though I'm quieter now, less enthusiastic about sharing and more focused on integrating. Spirituality, knowledge, and devotion are the anchors of my life, and they come naturally to me. But spirituality is a boring topic for a lot of people. Some say it is too heavy, too serious, impractical, and others wear the sign "Just Not Interested" on their face!

Some ask, "What is spirituality anyway?"

Some say that spirituality makes people lose their drive to succeed in life. Is that true?

Silicon Valley is full of successful people. It's noble to pursue success in life. Who will tell you to be a failure? But how you define success, how it's achieved, and with what attitude, is also important. People respect those who have done well through intelligence and hard work.

There's nothing wrong with earning money: it's quite useful, but at what cost? I definitely don't want a stressful job. I may not even realize that I have developed these traits! I don't want to sacrifice my conscience. No one respects those who have earned money using the wrong means or who have become arrogant from it. It nullifies everything. Would I be happy? Would I be healthy? I don't think so. I look at others and see how their health has deteriorated. Those chasing money, power, or fame are struggling feverishly to achieve it, fretting to maintain it in fear of losing it, and then suffering great misery when it starts going away. In this entire cycle, meant to eventually and inevitably achieve happiness, where and at what point does one feel satisfaction or joy?

So then how do I do well without becoming greedy, jealous, egoistic, arrogant, selfish, or addicted to money?

Here's one of my favorite jokes:

A top executive on vacation at a Mexican beach watches a fisherman get up late every day, work a few hours, eat lunch, sleep in the afternoon, and party in the evening with his amigos (friends).

The ambitious executive is very restless so he asks the fisherman: Why do you go fishing only for a few hours?

Fisherman: I earn enough for my family; I'm happy...

Executive: Well, you can work double the number of hours, earn double, get another boat, then two, then open a company...then take the company public...then you will be rich!

Fisherman: Okay. How long will that take?

Executive: About ten to fifteen years.

Fisherman: After all that hard work, then what?

Executive: Then you can retire!

Fisherman: Retire and do what?

Executive: Then you can get up late, do some fishing, eat, sleep, and party with your friends....

Yes of course we should work hard, during our working years, earning money to support our family. The lazy want easy money, to make the most but do the least. There are some who take the easy route in life, like a man who marries the only daughter of a rich man and then doesn't work another day in his life. He doesn't get much respect from his wife, children, or relatives, but he doesn't care. He is so lazy that he doesn't even help with anything at home or with the kids. He gets up late, reads the newspaper, eats, sleeps, and hangs out with friends. What a waste of human life!

There are some very interesting people in the world who are good examples of what *not* to be. I think perhaps some of the worst of them are the corrupt Indian public officials and their partners in crime. I know them well. If there is a definition for demon, they would fit it exactly. They are a disease in society. The whole country is suffering from their sins. Yes, they, too, have an undying thirst for money and power, any way they can get it, even if it's illegally or immorally. What's the point of such money? People often justify their wrongdoings, saying, for example, that "Everyone is doing it, and why should I miss out?" Unfortunately for India, these corrupt politicians and bureaucrats are the dominating driving force.

In short, three examples of what not to do are clear to me. My actions should not be driven by unending selfish desires, nor should I pursue my goals using illegal or immoral means, and I definitely should not be lazy. And this is the gist of the second verse of the *Isha Upanishad*.

As Buddha also said, the cause of grief is desire. Greed, ego, and craving lead only to self-destruction. I firmly believe that, even though it may not seem like that in the short term. This is also said in the third verse in the *Isha Upanishad*.

Then what *is* the right attitude for doing well in the world?

Vedic wisdom teaches us that spirituality is not antagonistic to success. Two of the four goals of life (*Purushartha*) are material prosperity (*Artha*) and fulfillment of desires (*Kama*) to sustain oneself. But the only sustainable way is through *Dharma*— through moral, legal, and healthy means, without greed, lust, jealously, ego, anger, etc. *Dharma* is all about desire management. The Vedic wisdom says awake, arise, realize your potential! There's nothing wrong with being a rich business owner, a famous celebrity, or a powerful President. Finally, it's not about how much you have but how content you are.

There is a good example of this in history. Long ago there lived a very powerful king with a huge royal treasury. He held the responsibility for his large kingdom very well. He was very just and kind to his people, so they loved him. He was a role model for all. He was rich, powerful, and famous. But he was also a spiritual king, wise and skillful. His name was Krishna. He taught his friend, prince Arjun, how to be successful while being spiritual, such as not to drop his role or duties and run away into the forest and meditate. He guided him on the principles of Karma Yoga, how to excel in the materialistic realm through righteous actions and a noble attitude. That would lead him to the ultimate goal of being a better, wiser person.

Let me explore this Wisdom in Action that Sri Krishna explained to Arjun; let me give it a chance. It may make my life better, happier, and more successful. What do I have to lose? Firstly, I should not assume it's hard to practice. It may be a better option than being greedy, lazy, or immoral. So I read chapters two, three, four, and five of the Bhagavad Gita. Definitely a very good guide for life. Chapter Two, which is like a summary of the Gita, verse forty-seven famously says this:

> "*Karmanye vadhikaraste ma phaleshu kadachna. Karmaphalehtur bhurma te sangostv-akarmani.*"
> *Thy right is to work only, but never to its fruits; let the fruit-of-action not be thy motive, nor let thy attachment be to inaction.*

Which basically says the key to happiness is have a goal, give 100 percent effort, but drop the desire for the results. If you've done that, then there are no regrets either. Usually the desire for a result drives our actions and we end up either unhappy or wanting more. Like a rat on a wheel, we are stuck in this endless cycle.

If I could do my best in life, but from a sense of service (*Seva*) and duty toward my family and our society, and not just for myself, then there will be no greed, no insatiable selfish desires. Makes sense, right? I could achieve the max I can in life and at the same time offer all I do to the divine, and take whatever is the outcome as His offering to me; there would be no desires (I want...), no ego bragging (I did this), no selfishness claiming (this is mine), and no attachment—and therefore no misery. No matter how much wealth, power or fame I get, I will have no side effects from them; I will enjoy them with a sense of renunciation.

When I look at them from a broader perspective, if I realize that everything is God, that it's all Him, then He is doing and achieving everything, not me. I am not the doer.

So I have to purify my mind and emotions. When I'm free of anger and ego, the world will seem like a better place, and I will be happy. I have to change, not others. There's a Michael Jackson song I really like called "I'm talking about the man in the mirror. I'm asking him to change his ways. No method can mend and deliver. If you want to make the world a better place, take a look at yourself, and make that change."

Gandhi-ji also said, "Be the change you want to see in the world."

As I change, so will the world.

But what if I don't change? What happens if I keep doing things that are driven from some desire, to satisfy my ego, to gain something as a result?

I will be trapped in the endless cycle of *Samsar:* of birth and death, happiness or unhappiness, like being stuck a giant wheel going up and down endlessly. When we act from our desires it creates certain patterns, impressions and tendencies in us called *Vasanas*. The oldest patterns in us are those of eating, having sex, and fear. They are the hardest to get rid of. These tendencies create desires. For example, if we have a tendency to eat sweets, it will create a desire to eat desserts. Then we will act upon these desires and eat sweet things. The memory of the enjoyment will deepen the tendency, which will again lead to desires in an endless cycle. These patterns and impressions carry on from lifetime to lifetime.

That's why we need to reduce these patterns and bad habits through Wisdom in Action—acting with awareness and dispassion. Anyway, nothing is permanent, right? Money, titles, jobs, houses, and cars come and go. They are ours only for a short while. Whose wealth is it, anyway? Then why should I be so attached to them? It will only bring misery. Sometimes on the road someone will race past me and the next thing I see is that they are waiting at the next red light next to me. We can keep racing through life but we'll all end up in the same place, in a pot full of ashes!

Extra credit:

They say a picture speaks a thousand words. The image of the Bhagavad Gita with Krishna and Arjun on the chariot in the battlefield says so much. The chariot, in modern times, can be replaced by a car and its parts.

Symbolism:

1. Chariot: The physical body, the instrument through which the Self, intellect, mind, and senses operate.
2. Charioteer: Krishna represents the Self/soul/ consciousness, is supposed to be the wise giver of instructions to the mind.
3. Passenger: Arjun represents the individual Soul, the embodied Atma, the pure center of consciousness, which is always the neutral witness.
4. Horses: Sensory organs, such as eyes (vision), ears (hearing), nose (smell), tongue (taste), and skin (touch), through which we relate to the external world by perception and action.
5. Reins: Mind, through which the senses receive their instructions to act and perceive.
6. Roads: The countless objects of senses and desires in the world and in our memory.
7. Wheels of the chariot: right effort.
8. Destination: "Perfection" or "Self-realization."
9. Kurukshetra battlefield: the inner battlefield, the only place where one can confront, do battle with, and vanquish the inner demons.
10. Two armies: One hundred Kauravas represents one hundred demonic tendencies and the five Pandavas, the

five divine virtues.

The battle (*Mahabharat*) is still going on every day within us; this is the fight between our demonic and divine qualities. There has always been a struggle between the two. In this conflict between opposing forces, consciousness (Krishna) is ever on the side of righteousness (Dharma), the reality that sustains, not the delusion that undermines. With the guidance and wisdom (Gita) from one who has merged with consciousness (Krishna) I can overcome the one hundred inner negative tendencies with only five inner divine virtues. Then this chariot is to be driven to the destination that is Self-realization. It is the same on the outside macrocosmic level also. In the world I find the ration of good people to bad people as 100:5.

4 TAKE A DEEP BREATH IN AND LET GO!

"Oooooooommm...Shanti...Shanti...Shanti." Sri Sri Ravi Shankar is just finishing a meditation at a public event. He is one of the foremost spiritual masters in the world today.

An interviewer is asking people after the event: "What are your thoughts on meditation?"

"Nah, I don't want to meditate, I'm fine!" "Can't imagine closing my eyes and sitting still for so long." "Yeah, I meditate but not regularly; guess I need to be more disciplined." "Oh, yes, of course I meditate, everyone should meditate!" "Why do people meditate?" "I want to, but don't know how." "What *is* meditation?"

Boy, there's a whole range of questions and opinions on meditation.

The most ironic thing in the world is that everyone wants peace of mind but doesn't have it when it's truly needed!

I am not a great meditator or anything. Spiritual masters are established in meditation, they don't need to sit with their eyes closed and meditate. They *live* in meditation.

I was taking a walk yesterday evening in my complex. Earphones on, playing my favorite devotional songs. I started off with my thoughts on the list of things I had to do on Monday. We live in complex that has lots of trees, on a hillside, with open green areas and kids playing. As I listened to a soothing devotional song, I started to enjoy the nature walk through the tall evergreens. The sun was going down, the sunlight getting softer, birds getting their evening meal, and there was a gentle breeze. All of nature was in its own rhythm. It was so calming to be in sync with the harmony in nature, I took a deep breath and smiled, soaking it all in. Well, that wasn't meditation, but it felt good!

I keep learning and experiencing, and I can also take a step back and observe my journey so far. So many wonderful realizations come through me; it's hard to write them all down. Recently I was thinking about the three phases of evolution of the the individual soul (*Jiva*). My thoughts were that the first phase in human evolution is the removal of impurities (*Tamas*) and that is through the Yoga of Action (*Karma Yoga*). Then we are brought to the second phase which is to go beyond restlessness (*Rajas*). For this we need to go through the Yoga of Practice (*Upasana*), i.e., Pranayama (Yoga of breath), meditation, Yoga, worship, devotion. This settles the restlessness. Finally, we are taken to purity and clarity (*Sattva*) that come through the Yoga of Knowledge (*Jnan*). It is the last phase of an individual soul's evolution (*Vedanta*) and this takes the seeker to the other shore. This unfolding doesn't take place in one lifetime, but over lifetimes.

What is amazing is that once a person has completed a phase, she is transported into the next phase. Nature creates a conducive environment, with events and situations that make it happen. I have just realized this as an aha! moment in my life. I went through a phase of restlessness and spiritual practices over many years and now I've been picked up and placed into an environment of purity and knowledge.

I feel that the Yoga of Action phase is also to settle the account of previous mistakes (Karma theory in Vedic wisdom). If we didn't fulfill the duties as a student in a previous life, we will come back in another life and be presented with the same situation in which we need to fulfill those duties. It's like we failed in fifth grade and now we need to repeat it. This is also linked to tendencies and patterns. Suppose you have a deeply ingrained tendency to be lazy. You will continue to be faced with problems related to laziness until you we overpower our tendency through the Yoga of Action. *This is the transition from living with a mind driven by the wild horses of selfish desires and tendencies, to taming the mind with the wisdom and guidance of the scriptures (Vasana anusari to Shastra anusari).* Hence the mind is purified through the Yoga of Action. Of course first one needs to be aware that most, almost 80 percent, of our mind and actions are driven by patterns and tendencies *(Vasanas).*

I have been meditating for many years; I started spontaneously when I was a teenager without any proper instruction. Much later, I was initiated by a teacher in the Art of Living Foundation and given a secret personal *Mantra.* Recently, I decided to revisit meditation from the perspective of the ancient Vedas and the Bhagavad Gita. So I attended a workshop conducted by Swami-ji on meditation. Most ancient Vedic texts start with a seeker asking his Guru a question and then the teachings follow. Swamiji started with a list of questions most seekers have and that would be addressed during the seminar:

1. What is meditation? What meditation is not.
2. What to meditate upon. What is the purpose of meditation?
3. Who is the meditator?
4. How to meditate? The practice of meditation.
5. Obstacles in meditation.
6. Fruit of meditation.
5. Living in meditation. Description of a realized soul. How a wise one lives in the world. (This part I loved!)

Pre-requisites

The Bhagavad Gita's first few chapters are on *Karma Yoga.* Swamiji explained the purpose of *Karma Yoga* and its importance for meditation. Can we truly settle the mind if the mind is not purified first through Yoga of Action? Yes, but the calm will be achieved only to the extent that the negativity has been removed. We will be peaceful while meditating and still have negativity later. I have seen many people, including myself, who have been meditating for years, some for more than twenty years, but they still have so much ego, anger, and other negativity in them. So the cup of the Knowledge (*Jnan*) can't be full until the cup of Practice (*Upasana*) is full, and the cup of Practice can't be full until the cup of Action (*Karma*) is full. But no one phase is more superior than the other; each one is supreme. All three need to be done-the previous ones can't be abandoned, although the quality changes. For example, one who has gained wisdom serves the world (*Karma*) as an expression of love, still meditates and worships the Lord.

Disturbed mind - Vikshepa

Once the muddy and turbulent water is purified through Yoga of Action, Swamiji said, the next step is to calm the waters through meditation. Even if you are a good person, your mind may not be in control. The restlessness and turbulence is on the surface. We have so many distractions, and so many agitations and restlessness; the end result is discomfort and sorrow. This is called "*Vikshepa*," or disturbance. The cause of disturbance, or sorrow, is that the mind is craving something; there are hidden tendencies (*Vasanas*). Different people adopt different methods to get rid of this. These methods can be "*Tamasic*" (impure): alcohol, drugs, medication, but the sorrow doesn't go permanently-there's only temporary relief, and these methods bring more long-term problems like addiction and other side effects. "*Rajasic*" (passion, lust, greed) methods to remove sorrow include turning toward different kinds of entertainment, becoming a workaholic, keeping busy to avoid thinking about sorrow, and disturbances in the mind.

Then there is a "*Sattvic*" (pure) method to get rid of misery. The pure means are devotion to God, prayer, Yoga, meditation, being in the company of wise people, and listening to spiritual teachings to gain peace of mind. Pure methods don't produce new desires or have side effects.

Body-Mind-Intellect

We are told to eat a good diet and exercise to keep the body healthy. But what checks how much and what we eat, tells us to exercise, develops good habits, and has a say over the senses? A happy, healthy, strong, and disciplined mind. How can we tame the mind, bring it to rest at will, say 'No!' to the wrong thoughts, and teach it not to react? How do we manage the mind? So much happens in our mind: perceptions, beliefs, assumptions, expectations, feelings, and so on. Our goal is mind over body, but what directs the mind? Will power, awareness, intellect, wisdom, and conscience.

Prana-yama

As a preventative measure, we can curb our desires internally by gaining wisdom and expanding our awareness, and externally through Karma Yoga. But if we still end up doing things driven by selfish cravings, attachment, and ego, then the consequence will be that we have residue in the form of negative emotions. The cure or purification of negative emotions can be done through Pranayama. Pranayama is a Yoga technique that uses rhythms in the breath to affect the mind, as body, breath, and mind are connected.

So we can purify our feelings and emotions through the breath. Also, when the '*Prana*,' or life force, is high, we have a positive mind, and when the *Prana* is low, we have negativity. Yoga and Pranayamas have to be taught and checked by a Guru, a Yoga master.

33

Pranayamas and other Yoga methods are *Tantra*. What is *Tantra*? *Tantra* means technique. So the techniques in Kriya Yoga for examples fall under this category, as do other techniques that deal with 'life force' or 'energy.'

Pranayama, like other techniques, *naturally leads the mind into meditation*. Some people don't even realize that they are in a meditative state when this happens.

Body – If you have done Yoga or had a good work out and then you sit in the sauna, the mind is ripe for meditation.

Breath – Pranayama as mentioned.

Senses – You can have an intense experience through one of the senses that can take you into meditation. Imagine, for example, observing the vast expanse of the sea, or lie down and look up into the stars. In these situations, the mind expands, transcends.

Emotions – If you are listening to a devotional song, and go into bliss, it leads to meditation.

Intellect – If you have heard some deep knowledge and you sit and reflect on it, you can go into meditation.

Meditation happens in the transition between thoughts. Actually meditation happens, you can't do it. You can only create a congenial atmosphere for it to do so.

But there is a procedure for meditation. Sit comfortably with the spine erect and head straight. Close the eyes and relax the body, take a deep breath in…and let go…Drop the world, observe the body, let the mind be…sink into the substratum…

First, the chain of thoughts that make the mind flow outward need to make a U-turn and become focused. Worshiping a form of the Lord helps; repeating the name of the Lord (*Japa*), sometimes on a necklace of beads; helps merge the thoughts with love on the divine. But meditation is not concentration, and this is elaborated upon in one of the greatest texts on Yoga philosophy, the Yoga Sutras by Sage Patanjali. It describes the eight steps of Yoga that lead to Samadhi, or oneness, and this takes us to the final goal of liberation called *Kaivalya*. The text goes into the details of Yoga and meditation.

The way to succeed in the world is with effort, and the way to succeed at meditation is through letting go, making it effortless, and being natural. It is just *being*. In the Upanishads and Gita it says that I should sit in meditation with the attitude of renunciation, *Sanyaas*. No matter what is happening in my life, no matter what I'm thinking. Who cares? Leave it, let me repose in myself.

Panch Kosha - the five sheaths of our existence

Meditation is like peeling away the layers of an onion, moving from the outside, in. Starting from the environment around us and being at peace with it, dispassionate about everything happening around us. The sounds, the smells, everything. The eyes are closed. Then being aware of the whole body, having reverence for the body, relaxing the body. Then becoming aware of the inflow and outflow of the breath. Strange as it may seem, we are not aware of the breath, even though we are always breathing! The breath is always in the present moment. When the mind is in the present moment it becomes calm and crystal clear. Then becoming aware of the mind, aware of the thoughts, witnessing the thoughts coming and going, like watching a river flowing by. Being aware of each thought. The mind settles, thoughts decrease. Then there is a feeling of peace, harmony, joy, love, expansion.

Sometimes when I meditate it feels really sweet, and that is very addictive. However, that is not the final stage of meditation. I still "feel"; it is still the mind enjoying the nectar of the innermost layer. I want to see my soul, I am determined, steady...steady... Finally, silence. The final state is that of no-mind and absolute bliss. You are now completely your true, natural Self. Going beyond all the layers and returning to the core takes practice, patience, steadfastness, and dispassion.

As stated before, we are all looking for this bliss in many ways. We want to return to our original state. Alcohol can make you happy, but then you have submitted your mind to it; those chemicals rule your mind, making you a slave, and then the effect finally goes away, and you feel down. In meditation you rule the mind, and that bliss is always available to you. It never leaves, never diminishes, never changes. Just being in the bliss that we *are* is meditation. *This is why we should meditate.* In our everyday lives we are removed from our state of natural bliss, but saints are always established in this bliss. They function from this state. In meditation, it permeates us, it is in every cell, like water in a sponge. Actually, even the sponge is solidified consciousness.

Mantra - the sacred-secret sound.
There is an ancient tradition in which a spiritual Guru initiates a student by whispering a sacred Mantra for meditation. A suitable mantra is chosen for the student based on the vibration in the sound of the mantra, and the meaning is not the important part. There is a vibration that resonates with each of the seven *Chakras*, the energy centers in our body. This sacred sound of the mantra is like a seed that is placed within and that then grows as it resonates. It is repeated mentally during meditation. The vibrations of the sound rise up and then expand like ripples on a pond. When there are thoughts, the vibration of the mantra consolidates them into a single sound, like ripples bring synchronicity to scattered disturbances on the surface of water. The vibrations settle, and the mind dives into deeper and deeper layers of consciousness, like sinking into the ocean under the waves of thoughts. If thoughts come, repeating the mantra brings oneness

to the mind, and the vibration of the mantra dissolves the thoughts. When the vibration settles there is absolute silence, stillness, and deep rest. The mind dissolves into the vast expanse of consciousness.

Sri Krishna gives Arjun guidance on meditation and describes its results in the sixth chapter of the Bhagavad Gita. Nowhere else in the entire extent of the voluminous spiritual literature that we have in the Upanishads, the Brahma Sutras and the Bhagavad Gita (the three are known as the *Prasthana Traya*), can we find such a wealth of details, explaining not only the technique of meditation so vividly but also the possible pitfalls and how to avoid them successfully. It talks about the discipline of "Yoga", to control ones senses and desires, before getting into the practice of meditation.

Sri Krishna talks about the right attitude for meditation. You should mentally prostate to your spiritual teacher or Guru (if you don't have one, then the God you believe in). Next, think about God (Allah, Jesus, Buddha, Krishna, or whoever is your God), single-mindedly. Consider the Self as the supreme goal of life when you sit in meditation. Withdraw the mind from the world with dispassion, and eliminate all distractions of the mind, slowly and patiently. Then draw the mind to the Self with determination. Contemplate on the nature of the Self, pure existence, consciousness, and bliss. The great gravitational force of the Self will pull the mind to Itself like a magnet. The mind, then, will dissolve into the Self like salt in the ocean.

Meditation is effortlessly abiding in the awareness of one's own true nature. It is about experiencing the source, tracing back to see where the "I" comes from. One morning during retreat, as I meditated, I asked myself, "Who am I?"..."Who is meditating?"..."Oh, who just asked this question?"..."This thought— where did it come from?" "Who is the meditator?"

Observing each thought come and go. Reposing in the silence between the thoughts. Being aware of the subtlest of thoughts. The response to these questions is a great experience.

Our soul is in the gap between the thoughts. Even a moment of no-mind without a trace of thought is like a deep dive into eternity, through a black hole where there is no time or space. Everything becomes one: the world vanishes, and there is no mind, only consciousness. When you come back, it feels like only a fraction of a second has passed, and when you observe things outside, you realize how much time has passed—you may have been "gone" over an hour! Great yogis can be in this state as long as they want. During meditation some people blink into this timelessness and think they went to sleep. If you are not drowsy, it can't be sleep—it's deep meditation.

First stage of practice is listening to knowledge on the nature of the Self. Then comes consolidating the knowledge, removing doubts, reflecting. The last stage is making it an experiential reality. In the Upanishads the term for meditation is *Nididhyasa*, which means the yearning for deep thinking. It is about turning the mind inward to the Subject - the Self, the *Atman*.

The experiences in meditation are hard to express, but here they are beautifully described in the words of Sri Krishna:

> *When the mind, restrained by the practice of Yoga, attains quietude and when seeing the Self by the self, he is satisfied in his own Self; (Gita, 6.20)*
>
> *When he (the Yogi) feels that Infinite bliss —- which can be grasped by the (pure) intellect and which transcends the senses —- wherein established he never moves from the Reality; (Gita, 6.21)*
>
> *Which, having obtained, he thinks there is no other gain superior to it; wherein established, he is not moved even by heavy sorrow.*

(Gita, 6.22)

Let it be known: the severance from the union-with-pain is Yoga. This Yoga should be practiced with determination and with a mind steady and un-despairing. (Gita, 6.23)

Supreme Bliss verily comes to this Yogi, whose mind is quite peaceful, whose passion is quieted, who is free from sin, and who has become Brahman. (Gita, 6.27)

The Yogi engaging the mind thus (in the practice of Yoga) , freed from sins, easily enjoys the Infinite Bliss of 'Brahman-contact. (Gita, 6.28)

With the mind harmonized by Yoga he sees the Self abiding in all beings, and all beings in the Self; he sees the same everywhere. (Gita, 6.29)

This is the Unity Consciousness state as described by some. The description of a realized one, established in the Self, is so beautiful and mesmerizing.

5 THE NECTAR OF LIFE

I feel that self-discipline needed for Yoga and meditation is easier for men than it is for women. Women being more emotional, devotion is an easier path to the same goal. Only with faith and devotion can meditation result in realization, in the revelation of truth. Worshiping the divine is a form of devotion, and devotion is the nectar of life. In fact devotion, or love, is our true essence, and everything in life is an expression of our love. So I need to realize this great love within me. What is the way back home? Is it through devotion and worship?

Like sweetness is to sugar, devotion is to me. The only reason I am in this human body is to experience devotion. Liberation I can gain even after I leave the body. Nothing exists in this world for me except for my beloved Krishna. The moment I remember Him, His presence is with me. My yearning becomes devotion, my conversations become poetry, and our union becomes bliss. Those who have experienced will understand; for those who haven't: I can't explain! Fortunate are those who in human birth have felt this devotion for the Lord.

The most beautiful expression of consciousness is devotion. God created a mirror to see His love, and the reflection was a beautiful maiden brimming with devotion. In this divine love God embedded the highest wisdom, an essence of Himself. Devotion is an intense longing for the beloved. It is the urge to merge with the divine. Devotion is intoxication with the nectar of divine love, the cup of the heart overflowing with bliss. Without the juice of devotion, all knowledge, all sadhana (spiritual practices) are dead and dry like sawdust. A perfect relationship has an equal balance of both love and respect. Devotion is that perfect relationship with the divine; it is the most intimate with the deepest reverence.

Love seeks devotion, devotion seeks bliss. I mistake these human emotions to be His love, like a mirage it glimmers in the hot dry sand, I chase it till I get tired, and exhausted I fall down. The moment my vision shifts to Him, *Giridhari*, that moment there is coolness, bliss. That instant there is freedom, expansion, relief, and my thirst is quenched! That emptiness inside is filled in an instant with immense love. No matter how much I try to express my love for Him it is incomplete. That strong urge for His presence, that pleading and prayer, my soul cries, "Oh Krishna! Be with me! Come to me my Govind Giridhari!" Tears of love and longing roll down my face...

I cannot remember a time when He was not part of my life. When I was a little girl I saw His painting at an exhibition, my *Kanhaiya* stealing butter from a pot with his friend. I was so mesmerized and lost in the painting that I forgot everything. When my parents looked around, they realized I wasn't with them; they found me staring into the painting! Krishna is my best friend.

If I were to think of all the precious moments in my life, a lot of them are connected with my Krishna. We were in Zambia, having just returned from a trip to India, and my mother had bought this statue of Krishna as a gift for someone. I vividly remember the day when I told my mother that I would like to keep that statue. I must have been around twelve. I used to hold that Krishna statue in my hand, put on Krishna bhajans, and sing and dance with Him. One day in my room He looked so alive in the statue, I asked Him, "Is it You? Show me a sign," and He did. I still have that sandalwood statue of Krishna.

So innocent, pure, and beautiful were those moments that I shared with Krishna as a little girl. I am still that little girl, and in my heart there is a sacred space in which there is only Krishna and my entire existence is within Him. Whenever I feel intense devotion or deep despair I hold his statue close to my heart, and looking at Him, I fall asleep.

Like the rays of the sun, each one's devotion is beautiful and unique.
Each one of us is a natural lover; it is the easiest thing to be...
Each one of us attempts to express it differently, yet love cannot be expressed fully...
Each one of us has a definition of love, at different times, for different people, but love cannot be defined...
Each one of us loves someone or something, so deeply, so passionately, but love cannot be found in the finite...

Where are You, my love, for whom I seek and for whom my soul cries? Since eons I have longed for you...
O my beloved, quench this thirst so I may merge with You and be One and Whole!
There is none other than You in all creation, this "I" will merge with the true me then roam free and high!
Till then I sing in a trance of love...Till then I dance in a play of love. The angels envy me; I am here in your company, and experience the colors of love in ecstasy!

At the pinnacle of devotion is liberation
At the pinnacle of knowledge is Divine Love
In Divine Love knowledge is inherent
Without love, knowledge is meaningless...

For a devotee, this duality is a play, but in the ultimate bliss of divine love the devotee merges into the divine and becomes One. For a wise one, there is no duality. He knows he is God—*Aham Brahmasmi*. No matter what the path, the journey ends in Oneness and the wise one realizes that He is Love, He is Knowledge. I feel Krishna as my soul! In my entire being. As a glow from within. Someone once asked me, "Where is your Krishna," and I replied, "He is always with me."

The Raas Leela of Krishna, Radha and the *Gopis* (devotees) symbolizes the eternal cosmic celebration of creation with consciousness, the dance of duality. Krishna is consciousness and the Gopis creation. Krishna is mine, only mine! Like those *Gopis*, I am dissolving in devotion...merging into my charming Krishna...oh! I am drunk with this bliss!—and in the height of this ecstasy I become unconscious; nothing remains, just His cool, divine loving presence. Leave me here; I am satisfied, I am finally at rest, my heart at home...

> The mind drops to the heart, becomes meditation...
> The heart longs...oh! My beloved...blossoms into devotion...
> These tears of devotion...become precious pearls...
> In the dance of trance un-become...merge...transcend...

Devotion is not to be explained or understood; devotion is a poem to be sung! Around the fifteenth century there was a burst of devotion with Sufis and saints singing love poems for the divine. Buddha was wise, enlightened, and complete. Devotional saints Chaitanya and Meera experienced ecstasy, danced, and sang, and they were also enlightened and complete. They experienced the highest state of devotion, "What am I without You?" They demonstrated that this body is capable of both wisdom and devotion.

Meera Bai

Meera Bai epitomizes Bhakti (devotion). Her unwavering love for her Krishna was the most beautiful. Even Krishna would helplessly be drawn to her. Her conversations with Krishna poured out as poetry, as love songs for the divine (*bhajans*). For a devotee, all love songs are *bhajans* (devotion songs), and all *bhajans* are love songs. Hers are remembered even today. She did not want to get married but was married to Rajasthan's Mewar kingdom's prince, Bhoj Raj, when she was thirteen. She was not interested in married life. For her, no one existed except Krishna. She spent most of her time in the temple and not at the palace with the family or nor did she behave like royal blood. Her husband died in war a few years after they married, when Meera was only sixteen. Meera's father-in-law liked Meera, and protected her from the other family members' insults. She must have been around nineteen when her father-in-law also died. Meera's older brother-in-law, mother-in-law and sister-in-law were very unjust to Meera and tortured her. They wanted her to maintain the dignity of the family and act like a princess, not have a daily communion with ordinary people to sing *bhajans* and behave like a commoner. She was also a rebel and an unconventional woman. She never let go of her devotion for Krishna, no matter how much anyone tried. In the bleakest time of her life, when her in-laws rebuked her and her own family didn't want her back, she sang the *bhajan*, "Mere to Giridhar Gopal dusaro na koi"—only Giridhar Gopal is truly my own and no other. I am wedded to that consciousness.

I don't know why her life was full of so much misery. Finally, when she was about twenty-one, she decided to leave her in-laws. One night, she left the fort of Chittaur with deep pain in her heart, mourning, "Why don't they understand that I love Him so much?" For many days, hungry and thirsty, she traveled through the desert. She spent some time in the birth town of Krishna, Mathura, and Vrindavan. She had always wanted to find a Guru and gain knowledge, but Saint Chaitanya's disciple in Mathura refused to initiate her into meditation, saying that she was a woman. To him she said, "I thought the only male in this universe is Krishna, the rest all female," meaning there is only one consciousness, Krishna, and the rest is all matter. She then went to Kashi and was initiated as a disciple by Saint Tulsidas. It was after this she sang, "Payoji maine Naam ratan dhan payo. Vastu amolik di mere Sat Guru, kiripa kar apanayo." "Naam" is when a Guru initiates a disciple with a *mantra* for meditation.

She finally went to Dwarka in Gujarat, which was the capital city of Krishna's kingdom. Sometime later, her youngest brother-in-law, Udai, built a new capital, Udaipur, with beautiful palaces, and wanted Meera Bai to come back. He sent a few people to Dwarka to convince her. She was happy in Dwarka and didn't want to go back. One night she entered the Dwarka Deesh temple, and in her supreme glory, her single-minded devotion for Krishna and intense longing to unite with him, she did. At that moment there was divine light. When the priests went in to look for her, all they found was her white Sari (garment). She left when she was around fifty.

If you asked me to choose between this love and knowledge, I would choose love. Knowledge seems so cold and dry and pales in comparison with the song, dance, and celebration with the divine! Come feel this ecstasy, the elation, the bliss when a lover merges with the beloved. It is electrifying. This, too, is *samadhi*—a sweet *samadhi*—not that emptiness.

Kabir

I love another saint of the fifteenth century, Kabir. He wrote simple, yet wise, poems that spur an individual to look for a deeper meaning to life.

Here is one of my favorite poems of *sant* Kabir:

Na Mein Dharmi Na Hi Adharmi Na Mein Jati Na Kaami Ho | Na Mein Kehta Na Mein Sunta Na Mein Sevak Swami Ho | |
Na Mein Bandha Na Mein Mukta Na Mein Virat Na Rangi Ho

| Na Mein Kahu Se Nyara Hua Na Kahu Ke Sangi Ho | |
Na Hum Narak Lok Ko Jaate Na Hum Swarag Sidhare Ho | Sab
Hi Karam Hamara Kiya Hum Karman Se Nyare Ho | |
Ya Mat Ko Koi Birla Bujhe So Atal Ho Baitha Ho | Mat Kabir
Kaho Ko Thape Mat Kahu Ko Mete Ho | |

Translation: Neither am I Righteous nor Non-Righteous
Neither am I an Ascetic nor a Sensualist | | Neither do I Speak
nor do I Listen Neither am I a Servant nor a Master | |

Neither am I Constrained nor Liberated Neither am I Sad
nor Jubilant | | Neither am I Distinctly Isolated from Anything
Nor am I Identified Completely with Anything | |

Neither do I go to the World of Hell Nor do I proceed to the
World of Heaven | | All Actions are really my Actions But yet
I am Distinct from the Actions | |

Sufis

Sufism is a devotional mystical dimension of Islam. Sufi poems
and music are close to my heart. I wish that this would once again
evolve in the Muslim culture. The wisdom embedded in the love
poems of the Sufis is beautiful and heart-moving. I listen to many
old Sufi poems and contemporary Sufi songs. Rumi is one of the
most revered Sufi saints, known for his mystic style. His poems
elegantly and consistently touch our inner being and inspire us to
go beyond our limitations towards the Divine. Rumi believed in
the religion of love.

Here are some Rumi quotes:

*"Your task is not to seek for love, but merely to seek and find all the
barriers within yourself that you have built against it."*
*"Knock, And He'll open the door Vanish, And He'll make you shine
like the sun Fall, And He'll raise you to the heavens Become
nothing, And He'll turn you into everything."*

"We come spinning out of nothingness, scattering stars like dust."

"This is love: to fly toward a secret sky, to cause a hundred veils to fall each moment. First to let go of life. Finally, to take a step without feet."

No emotion is more powerful or moving than love. The noblest kind of love is that which flows toward God, called love divine or devotion. Saints and sages affirm that deep within our hearts lies an undiscovered, infinite source of love that is without beginning and endless. Our scriptures reveal that through single-minded devotion we are led to our innermost sanctum, the higher Self, the source of all bliss and joy. But we tend to search for this infinite love in people, ideas, and objects. When this love is directed toward the higher, our vision expands and we see this divinity everywhere and in everything. In this way, we come to appreciate all of creation equally, enjoying lasting freedom and true happiness.

Eleven Manifestations of Devotion
Love cannot stand distance, and respect requires it. In devotion, love and respect are in perfect measure. A disciple or a devotee has intimacy as well as respect combined in one. The sage Narad in his Bhakti Sutras —The Aphorisms of Love—explains the eleven forms of devotion:

"Although devotional service is One, it becomes manifested in eleven forms of attachment: attachment to the Lord's glorious qualities, to His beauty, to worshiping Him, to remembering Him, to serving Him, to reciprocating with Him as a friend, to caring for Him as a parent, to dealing with Him as a lover, to surrendering one's whole self to Him, to being absorbed in thought of Him, and to experiencing the longing of separation from Him. This last is the supreme attachment." (Narada Bhakti Sutra, 5.82)

Worship - *Upasana*

Loving the aim you want to reach is worship.

And how am I to worship Him?

My hands are to serve Him, my heart to love Him, my voice to sing for Him, my eyes to behold His beauty, my ears to listen to His praise.

What can I offer to You that you already don't have? Ah! There is one thing you don't have…with all my love I surrender my ego to you. *Samarpayami*. With fullness in my heart and with folded hands I bow to the divine presence in my soul. I feel that immense overpowering love for Thee. There is only You, I do not exist. Let this form drop.

A saint once said: There are only two types of people in this world. One who believes in God and the other who worries. If you worry, you don't have true faith in God. Trust God. If you believe, have faith in God, you can't worry. There are some who worship God to ask something from Him, there are some who worship Him in gratitude, and there are some who know He is within them and everywhere, always, so they are ever blissful.

There is a beautiful prayer by Adi Shankaracharya, the prayer within for God, in which one verse reads:

"Aatmaa tvam girijaa matih sahacharaah praanaah shariiram griham Poojaa te vishhayopabhogarachanaa nidraa samaadhisthitih. Sajnchaarah padayoh pradakshinavidhih stotraani sarvaa giro Yadyatkarma karomi tattadakhilam shambho tavaaraadhanam.h .. 4"

Meaning: My soul is Your abode; may You manifest (divine mother) as my pure intellect, wisdom. My five vital airs are Your attendants, my body is Your abode, and all the pleasures of my senses are objects to use for Your worship. My sleep is Your state of transcendence. Each step I take in life is centered around You, everything I say may it be in praise of You, everything I do is in devotion onto You, o benevolent Lord!

The Ladder of Devotion - Gita

In the twelfth chapter of the Bhagavad Gita, Krishna talks about a ladder of Bhakti. The lowest rung of the ladder is: doing each action as an offering of a prayer to the divine; this is the Yoga of Action. Taking what comes as God's offering. Swamiji explained the "fruits of actions" well-he said 'fruits of action' is a technical term that means drop the worries and anxieties for the future. Keep your mind in the present; action is done in the present. If the mind is free from worries and anxieties then it is calmer and more focused and less divided to act. Worrying about the future takes away so much energy from the mind.

Here is the ladder of devotion from the first rung to the top most. When tendencies and impressions are 80 percent then drop the worries. This is when almost the entire ladder is still there to climb. When they become 60 percent (about halfway up), then do Yoga of Action, the mind and impressions get more purified. Then at 40 percent do spiritual practices, to bring back the wandering mind again and again. I think for that Pranayama and focus on breath is good. Then when 20 percent tendencies are there, the mind can be purified through meditation and contemplation.

Then Krishna explained that knowledge is more important than practices, meditation more important than knowledge. The highest form of devotion is meditation on the formless, the cosmic consciousness. And renouncing the fruits of action is more important than meditation. Peace immediately follows. This is the ladder of Bhakti. If you are confused it's okay.

There are different stages a devotee evolves through. First there is a need for a form, as the heart and mind are filled only in Him, and the devotee sees the divine in all forms and everywhere. The devotee then sees the divine as the essence behind all of creation and worships Him as the formless. As the devotee merges and dissolves she becomes one with the divine. This is the ultimate knowledge, and at the climax of devotion there is only this ultimate truth of Oneness.

Devotion is unconditional love between me and the divine, and at the peak of devotion, the merging into the divine, I *become* unconditional love, bliss.

6 GOD, GURU, AND SELF ARE SYNONYMOUS

Though devotion is natural to me, for Self-knowledge I need a spiritual master. Many years ago I wondered, who is a Guru? Why do I need a Guru? How will I know someone is the right Guru for me? Where will I find a Guru?

The world has been fortunate to receive the wealth of wisdom from great prophets and Gurus over the ages. I am grateful to my own Guru and all enlightened Gurus who have brought this eternal knowledge to us.

The first thing that the scriptures say is that we must have an enlightened master to take us to the goal of Self-realization. It is written in the Vedas, "*Acharyavaan Purusho Veda*," to attain Self-knowledge a person has to go to a teacher. Upanishad means sitting close to a master with an unshakable desire for Self-knowledge.

The East honors a tradition of Masters who have protected this eternal knowledge, and given this to us, generation after generation, according to the need of the age and time. It's depicted in one of my favorite movies, Star Wars, as the master and the apprentice. All Gurus, the Rishis of the Vedas, even Krishna, never claim that it's their knowledge but that, "We have heard from the wise ones," or "learnt it from my Guru." The knowledge has passed down from Guru to disciple for thousands of years. The first Guru, who was never a student, is *Narayana*, in the *Vaishnav* tradition, and *Dakshina Murthy*, in the *Shaivite* tradition. Initially the Vedic tradition was an oral tradition; the hymns and verses were recited by heart and passed down from teacher to disciples. It was much later that the great sage, Rishi Vyas, collected all the knowledge and codified it into the Vedas and other Vedic texts.

Vedic tradition emphasizes the need for a spiritual "Guru." If you were to read the Vedas independently, you would get hopelessly lost and confused. You would not be able to resolve the apparent contradictions and would either conclude wrongly or give up, thinking that it was too difficult or illogical. Therefore, Self-knowledge as revealed by the Guru is the means of Self-realization, similar to learning science from a science professor. But there is a difference between a scholar and a saint: that of the experience. A saint is a living example of Self-knowledge.

I can't meet Brahman/God, or converse with Him; how do I learn, ask questions, and interact with God? I would be lost if it was not for Gurus. In the past it was very common for each person, family, and king to have a spiritual Guru. The Hindi word "*Anaath*," commonly known as orphan, actually means one without a Guru, lost without wisdom.

For any learning to take place, three factors are required:

1. The object to be known.
2. The one who wants to know.
3. The means for knowing.

The most common means of knowing are:

a) Direct perception: It is the knowledge gained through the five sense organs of perception, e.g. eyes see color, form, etc.
b) Inference: Based on what we perceive and already know, we infer a thing. Example, we have experienced that wherever there is smoke there is fire. Therefore, on seeing

smoke we infer that there must be fire somewhere.

c) From what someone says. We gain knowledge by reading or hearing from people who have directly experienced a thing or heard about it. Both inference and knowledge of others are based on direct perception.

As regards Self-knowledge, the object to be known is the Self and the one who comes to know is also the Self. What are the means of knowing it? The Self is not available for direct perception, therefore it can't be inferred or spoken of. Then how is Self-knowledge possible? The means for it are through the revelations of enlightened beings, such as in the Vedas, and learnt through a Guru.

When that desire for being free is strong and sincere, a right master is given by nature. I may think that I can choose a Guru, but situations and events will happen such that I will approach the right teacher appropriate for my growth. Sometimes, as a seeker progresses and the present Guru is no longer appropriate for further growth, nature will bring forth another Guru who is suitable. Ramana Maharishi said

> "How is the Guru found? God, who is imminent, in His grace takes pity on the loving devotee and manifests himself according to the devotee's development. The devotee thinks that He is a man and expects a relationship as between two physical bodies. But the Guru, who is God or the Self incarnate, works from within, helps the man to see the error of his ways and guides him in the right path until he realizes the Self within."

A Guru need not be in physical form. When a qualified student asks a sincere question from a pure heart he will get the answer. Knowledge can be revealed from within and also from the whole world. When you are earnest about learning and growing, you can learn something from everyone, from every experience—good and bad—from nature, from everything all the time. However, the most progress is made from a realized master.

"Gu" means removal of the darkness of ignorance, and "Ru" means the light of Self-knowledge. Thus Guru means one who helps in moving from ignorance to the light of wisdom. Sri Sri Ravi Shankar says that a Guru is like a window, and the sky is like consciousness/God. To see the sky I need a window through which to see. As Ramana Maharishi said,

"The Guru does not bring about Self-Realization. He simply removes the obstacles to it."

There's a deep and subtle truth about a Guru. A Guru is one who *leads* a person to Self-realization. A Guru cannot give Self-realization to the disciple because it is the disciple who has to realize it. A horse can be led to a pond, but it cannot be made to drink water.

Sri Krishna says in the Gita:

"Uddharet atman aatmaanam Na aatmanam Avasaadhayet. Atmaiva hi atmano bandhuh Atmaiva ripuh atmanah."

Meaning, the Self has to help the Self and the Self should not degrade the Self. Because the Self is the friend of the Self and the Self is the enemy of the Self.

Hence a Guru will lead the disciple to the final step – but the final step is one the disciple has to take. A Guru helps the disciple in vanquishing or removing all the actions and their effects. Thus the mind of the disciple becomes pure. With spiritual practices like meditation the mind attains clarity. A mind that has acquired total purity and clarity is ready to absorb spiritual knowledge from a Guru. In a clear and pure mind, the Self shines easily.

Lastly, when the knowledge from a Guru is complete, the Self manifests itself as the Guru. This is beautifully expressed in the prayer to *Dakshina Murthy*:

> "Ishvaro Gururaatmethi Murthy Bheda VibhaagineVyomavad Vyaapta Dehaaya Dakshinamurthaye Namaha"

Self, Guru, and God – are one and the same thing with three different forms. To that *Dakshina Murthy* (who is the first Guru of all Gurus) who represents these three forms and who has a body all-pervading like space – I offer my salutations.

That connection, the oneness of Self and Guru, is what this ancient tradition of Guru and disciple is.

What is this connection? When a space ship travels towards the sun, it travels a certain distance and after that the gravity of the sun pulls it in. When a devotee is in the presence of the Master that gravitation is called "connection". Your Guru is your Self! The beauty of a living Guru is that he is a projection of my true Self, and I can see it clearly in front of me, I can interact with it. When I interact with my Guru, he not only reflects my thoughts and feelings, but also my true intentions, my inner most Self, and he communicates with my inner voice.

Just like you are connected to your forefathers through your living father, you are connected to all the great Gurus from time immemorial through your living Guru.

The Vedas describe two qualities of a Guru:

1. *Srotrajna*—Well-versed in scriptures. Not in the text, but knowing the import of the Vedas, which is nothing but about Brahman or Self. There are many layers of depth in this knowledge; a Guru knows the implied meaning that is

indicated by the literal meaning.

2. *Brahma Nishta* — Established in consciousness.

Only a teacher who is enlightened can lead the disciple to the doorway of the Self. Only one with experience of the Self can convey the knowledge of the Self, and this can be through mere presence, through silence. I don't see a Guru as a body, as a personality; I see the Guru as the presence of consciousness wrapped in a physical form. There is a magnetic connection—a subtle yet strong bond between the Atman and the enlightened one. A teacher can only raise a student to his level. A professor with a bachelor's degree can't teach a Ph.D. course to a student. If a Guru is a Siddha, a perfected yogi, he can raise a student only to his level, not to enlightenment. But how do I know if a Guru is enlightened? Only an enlightened one can recognize another enlightened being.

A true Guru is completely unselfish and devoted only to the evolution of the seeker. A Guru is like a mother who loves her disciple unconditionally. He takes you home and makes you meet your soul. There is a Sufi song which goes like this:

> *I felt a fragrance and followed, then got lost. It was a mirage but I kept chasing it. When I entered your doorway, only then did I get a vision of the truth. You made me meet the fragrance that was already within me.*
> *"Mujhme hi voh khushbu thi jisse tu ne milvaya"*

We have seen the nature of a teacher, a Guru. But what are the qualifications of a student to be accepted by a teacher, to know that he is ready for the highest knowledge?

7 DOORWAY TO KNOWLEDGE

Now that a Guru has been chosen for me, the next question is: Why do I need Self-knowledge? Do I need to be spiritual? I'm quite happy with my life, work, family, hobbies, and my devotion. So why do I need Self-knowledge?

Whatever I am inside determines the quality of my life outside. I see one who is established in knowledge, like a sage, as always happy, unaffected, free of anger, ego, and misery. So this is my goal—realizing the perfection within.

I have been learning for years from a teacher that I am consciousness, the Self, the Atman. But why has this not been my experience? Do I lack the ingredients that are the catalysts in realizing this knowledge?

What are these attributes that I need to develop to be a good student of Self-knowledge? Ah yes! They were described by Swamiji earlier as:

The four-fold qualifications for a seeker—*Sadhana-catushtaya*:
1. *Vivek:* discriminating wisdom on what is real/unreal, permanent/changing, Self/not Self, which leads to
2. *Vairagya:* Dispassion which leads to
3. The six spiritual wealths:
   Sama: mastery over the mind that leads to
   Dama: control over the external senses, that enables us to
   Uparati: withdraw from the world and do the right thing, i.e. *Dharma*
   Titiksha: have forbearance with the ups and downs of life.
   Shraddh: have faith in the scriptures and your Guru as the sources of knowledge on the unknown. All of the above

leads to,

Samadham: a focused mind that gets absorbed in the Self.

4. *Mumukshutva*: yearning for freedom. It is the desire to free oneself from all bondages by realizing one's true nature. I have to ask for a Guru to be given one. I have to ask for realization to be given, amazingly nature is listening it grants all true wishes, and miraculously I will gain it.

I have noticed that these qualities are both the requirements and also the outcomes of learning. I seem to have gained more *Vivek* and *Vairagya* over the years.

There are six philosophies in the Vedic tradition. I believe they are a progression in the evolution of understanding and not parallel paths. They are:

1. *Samkhya*
2. *Yoga*
3. *Nyaya*
4. *Vaisheshika*
5. *Mimamsa*
6. *Vedanta* - often refers to the last segment of knowledge in the Vedas, i.e. the Upanishads, and the last six chapters of Bhagavad Gita. It is the culmination of knowledge.

The first step in learning is to purify the mind through Yoga of Action, second is to attain clarity through spiritual practices (*Upasanas*). Swamiji says that the last phase of the spiritual evolution, Vedanta, is to lift the veil of ignorance (*Aavarna*) that is covering the true Self. This can only be done through gaining the knowledge of the Self.

The practice (*Sadhana*) for final liberation in Vedanta is to first listen to Self-knowledge from a Guru (*Sravanam*). Then reflect on this knowledge (*Mananam*) using one's intellect to remove doubts and answer questions that may arise. This leaves no conflict or confusion in the mind. You gain total clarity of knowledge. The final stage is to abide in the Self through meditation (*Nididhyasa*), the only way to experience the Self or consciousness. This practice is done repeatedly with patience and perseverance. In due time, depending on the inner qualities of the student, the veil drops forever. With the grace of God, when the fruit is ripe it falls. The self-effulgent soul shines forth like Buddha—the enlightened one!

Tattva Bodha

Before you read research papers on science, you have to go through the elemental studies of physics, chemistry, etc. In the same way it is good to learn the fundamentals on which the highest knowledge is based. One of the introductory texts on Vedic wisdom is the "*Tattva Bodha*," by Adi Shankaracharya. It covers the above and much more. It talks about the structure of creation and relation to consciousness. This chart (overleaf) graphically illustrates this part of the text:

It is interesting how the microcosm, the human being, is an exact replica of the macrocosm. The macrocosm replicates itself infinitely, like a fractal. An easy way to remember this is using the ten fingers. The five fingers on the right hand, pinky for physical body, ring finger for subtle body, index finger for causal body, fore finger for conditioned consciousness (*Jiva*) and thumb for soul (*Atma*). Then on the left hand, pinky for the total physical universe or creation(called *Virat*), ring finger for the total subtle creation or cosmic mind (called *Hiranyagarbha* or *Mahat Tattva*), index finger for the causal cosmic creation (*Mool Prakritri*), fore finger for the cosmic creator (*Ishvara*), and thumb for cosmic consciousness (*Brahman*). In addition to the associations made above, *Karmas* (account of our actions) and *Vasanas* (impressions) are part of the causal body. All the terms in the

Tattva Bodha in a nutshell
A visual presentation of the text

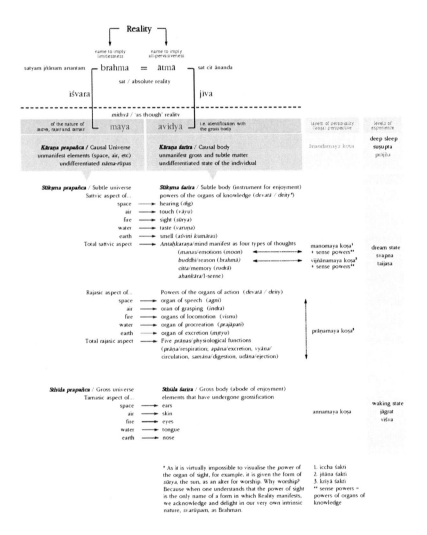

chart above such as *Isvara, Jiva, Maya*, etc. are explained in the
Tattva Bodha. *Jiva* is essentially the same as *Maya*, illusion. It is
the **veil of ignorance** that covers the true Self. It is the false
identification with the causal, subtle and gross bodies that get
conditioned and therefore *Jiva* is the conditioned consciousness.
The root cause of ignorance creates a sense of separateness, the

limited identity, the "I"ness, commonly known as ego. The gross body drops at death but the other bodies still exist and carry into the next birth. Once one is enlightened the *Jiva* also drops and there is no false separateness. The soul is seen as a part of the whole.

The text also gives an introduction to other Vedic concepts such as the theory of *Karma*, the description of an enlightened person, etc. I think the knowledge in the Tattva Bodha is very important, a pre-requisite for understanding any further teachings in the Vedic scriptures on creation and consciousness. This book is also available online as an eBook.

The house of the Self has many doors. If you're a feeler you can enter through the doorway of devotion. If you're a doer you can walk in through the path of right action. If you're a thinker you can enter through the gateway of knowledge. Even though one aspect may be dominant, they all exist in each other. Each path is supreme, each one leads to a flavor of enlightenment. Consciousness has created a beautiful diversity of great souls like Meera-devotion, Buddha-knowledge, and Mother Teresa-right action—each an example of using a different doorway to the Self. The Bhagavad Gita points this out in chapter thirteen, verses twenty-five and twenty-six:

"Some, by meditation, behold the Self in the Self by the Self; others by the "Yoga-of-Knowledge" (by Sankya Yoga) ; and others by Karma Yoga.

Others also, not knowing this, worship, having heard of it from others; they too, cross beyond death, if they would regard what they have heard as their Supreme Refuge."
- Bhagavad Gita. Ch 13 v 25-26.

They all lead to Self-knowledge, to the experience of the Self, and existential reality (your own nature).

Now I'm at the doorway of knowledge! I am ready to offer my body, mind, and ego into the sacrificial fire of the soul. Once I enter, where will I pass? Without my ego, who or what will I become? Tell me, oh, great soul— what is thy nature? I have read the great ones proclaim that it's a futile exercise trying to explain your nature. Only indications can be given. What lies on the other side of this veil called *Jiva*? Have I visited there before? Will I still exist with a body, mind, and "I"? With great faith in my teacher and scriptures I surrender to the unknown—ready to merge into infinitude. I want to know my soul. With great reverence I plead, "O Guru! Please accept me as your humble student, let me enter the house of self-knowledge."

8 NATURE OF THE SOUL

What is the Self? For a seeker it would be good to first know the nature of the consciousness, as described by the scriptures, before attempting to realize it. It must be explained by a Guru who has experienced the vision of his true Self. Since the Self cannot be known as an object of knowledge, it has to be revealed by subtle indicative methods.

The "Atma Bodha", by Adi Shankaracharya is a great introductory text on the nature of the soul. So why do I need to know the nature of the Self?

"Compared with all other forms of (spiritual) discipline, knowledge of the self it the one direct means for liberation" - Atma Bodha, v 2.

There are two ways to knowing the nature of consciousness:

1. Through negation or what it is not
2. Indicating what it is.

The soul is not the body, breath, mind, feelings, emotions, intellect, memory, or ego, which are related to the gross, subtle, and casual bodies. Our biggest fallacy is that we identify ourselves with one or more of these. Through negation I can become aware that I am not the body, I am not the mind, I am not the intellect, I am not the ego...On deeper reflection you can see that there is a witness to all of these. With single-minded awareness, take yourself to the source of thought, the source of "I." There is nothing beyond, yet it is the source of all logical thinking, etc. Amazing.

"Just as luminosity is the nature of the Sun, coolness of water and heat of fire, so too the nature of the Atman is Eternity, Purity, Reality, Consciousness and Bliss," the *Atma Bodha* continues in verse twenty-four. And

I am other than the body and so I am free from changes such as birth, wrinkling, senility, death, etc. I have nothing to do with the sense objects such as sound and taste, for I am without the sense organs.

I am other than the mind and hence, I am free from sorrow, attachment, malice and fear, for "HE is without breath and without mind, Pure, etc.," is the Commandment of the great scripture, the Upanishads.

I am without attributes and actions; Eternal (*Nitya*) without any desire and thought (*Nirvikalpa*), without any dirt (*Niranjana*), without any change (*Nirvikara*), without form (*Nirakara*), ever-liberated (*Nitya Mukta*) ever-pure (*Nirmala*).

Atma Bodha, v. 32–34

In each Upanishad and in the Bhagavad Gita the nature of the Self is revealed. So our true nature is existence, consciousness, bliss (*Sat–Chit–Anand*). Volumes have been written on this, but how to realize it? Only in meditation can consciousness be experienced.

In the thirteenth chapter of the Bhagavad Gita, Sri Krishna says something very interesting. From the eighth verse we get a description of the elements of "Knowledge" and they include moral qualities and ascetic practices that are conducive to spiritual awakening. A realized soul has all these beautiful traits, and conversely, if we let these virtues blossom in us, they will lead to self-knowledge. The first two virtues are "humility" and "modesty," essentially the absence of Ego. All the preparation so far in the path prescribed by this wisdom has been to eliminate selfishness and Ego. Of course being simple and natural is the antidote to ego. There is one other beautiful virtue that melts the ego—love. In unconditional love there is no ego. Love is the nature of the Soul. Not in small measure, but that infinite love "I am." I do believe all noble virtues such as compassion, humility, and dispassion are already present in me, some still in seed form. Let them grow and blossom in the garden of the soul. When they flower, let their fragrance touch the hearts of all. I will make a garland and offer them to the Lord.

When I think of compassion and unconditional love, the person who exemplifies it in my life is my mother. For me, my mother is a living goddess, Devi Lakshmi, the epitome of compassion. It isn't possible to put her love in words, let it be in my heart, it is too sacred to be written. Compassion also emanates from the unconditional love that we are. It is compassion and kindness that make us human. There is no point in being supposedly spiritual and not being compassionate. Those who are compassionate are spiritual in practice.

Life flows through the heart. It cascades like a waterfall through all the other faculties needed. This life force utilizes the mind and intellect as and when needed and has access to infinite knowledge and intuition. This flow of the river of life expands outwards infinitely as compassion. I feel it radiating like ripples from my heart.

If I live from my mind and intellect then this life force doesn't flow. I'm stuck in my head and in my ego, and thoughts veil my heart. I have used so much intellect in my life that now I need to turn the switch. To understand Vedic scriptures requires a lot of intellect; however, when spiritual knowledge dawns it purifies the intellect! There is so much *Rasa* in these Vedic texts. *Rasa* loosely translates to divine nectar. It is not like science where everything is an object, everything is cut and dried. In Vedic knowledge, everything is alive; the whole creation is a living organism. All Vedic scriptures are written as poems and sung in various rhythms, and there's that heart aspect to it, so that the knowledge has both the intellectual aspect (left brain) and the creative aspect (right brain).

For someone like me, whose existence is focused so much within, it's important to bring balance by being aware about the outside. There needs to be this balance inside and outside. As I was telling my son, inside you need to feel freedom, devotion, and compassion; outside you need to be energetic, dynamic, and skillful. I have spent lifetimes with the journey inward. Our Vedic scriptures talk so much about turning inward and focus a lot on the individual; this has made me disconnect somewhat from the world. Now that I focus on the outside world I realize there's a lot to learn!

I need to express my compassion, which I take for granted I already have, or I am. Only this can overcome a lot of my short-comings in dealing with people, in overcoming my anger, etc. Now that I am bringing attention and awareness to engaging with people and situations, it's bringing so much knowledge and happiness. It makes me see the life force within others. If only each one could only see this life force within all, and the same life force everywhere, we would do away with so much conflict and hatred. Compassion has made me happy as it has improved my relationships.

What I project is exactly what gets reflected back to me. Even a hint of negativity comes back to me as conflict. When compassion flows to another, the other person responds in peace, with love. Amazing!

So I need to live, act, and speak from the heart, all the time. I tell my son, "Do this. Do that. You didn't do this. Have you done this? Why didn't you do this?" So much in the head, focused on what needs to be done, that everything needs to be perfect, not letting go. So his reaction also comes from the head, heartlessly. And if I move from the heart, speak with love and sweetness, saying, "*Beta* (son) did you do this? Can you please do this? I know you must be tired, so much to do and remember. But you're so much better; you're such a wonderful son. Love you!" Then he also responds with so much love, wow! And there is a connection! Our hearts are bonded. Rajshree (an Art of Living Foundation teacher) told me once that I need to work on connecting with people. She said, "You need to do that nu-nu na-na with people." Meaning I've got to be nurturing, caring, and spoiling people with my love, like a woman, a mother, a wife, should be. I'm working on it...

I am so focused on knowledge, on being perfect, on content (as Rajshree said). But knowledge is embedded *in* compassion!

So much anger comes in seeing imperfection in people and situations; it makes one imperfect in the process, doesn't it? So much conflict comes in seeing right and wrong in people, their opinions, and their actions. Compassion is more important than right or wrong, though. Like Rumi writes: "Out beyond the field of wrong doing and right doing there is a field, I'll meet you there." With compassion, it's possible to bring about change in the imperfect without resistance, reaction, and conflict. Isn't it?

Compassion is needed *because* people are imperfect, even the most cruel and evil person. Compassion is to see through their imperfections and see that human within, who is just like me. I am also imperfect, yet I still love my inner core, which is perfect, knowing this brings compassion for me and others. When that tenderness comes in the heart, I will see just that pulsating life in everyone and realize we are all the same. The more compassion I have, the more humanness I see in the other person, his ignorance, imperfection, and negativity as his suffering so how can I react to him?. To the level I am centered in compassion, I am comfortable with imperfections in people and situations. That brings peace of mind, happiness, and freedom. Sri Sarada Devi (wife of Ramakrishna Paramahansa), an enlightened being, also called the Holy Mother by her disciples, was an embodiment of compassion and the love of a mother. Her last words were: "I tell you one thing. If you want peace of mind, do not find fault with others. Rather see your own faults. Learn to make the whole world your own. No one is a stranger, my child; the whole world is your own."

If only I could love everyone as One, as small mirrors reflecting the same creator. Love has meaning when I love the life in the other; otherwise it's just an emotion. What beauty this love has! Love has an ability to connect with every heart instantly without a spoken word, with just an immense presence, and a flood of sweet nectar. With this love and compassion I break free from this cage, and I find I can bring so many smiles, so much happiness, light up someone's eyes, just by the mere presence of this compassion! In each eye I see, it's me, it's me everywhere! Like a light among lights, a drop among drops of this ocean. My heart speaks the language of love, each cell brimming with ecstasy! Only with love does life become a song, only with this song does life become a dance! I dance in this imperfect world— untouched! I smile; I see life everywhere like an ocean, our bodies just like shells, with life within and life without. I am always at home!

Compassion should be the foundation on which the pillars of knowledge are built. Love should be the basis of all expressions of existence. Established in compassion, you should have dispassion. These two bring out your best skill in dealing with problematic people and situations.

Compassion doesn't mean accepting injustice from others. Krishna tells Arjun that it's your Dharma (duty) to fight for justice and it's Adharma (unrighteous) to take injustice; in fact, it's stupid, and very few people realize this.

Compassion naturally expresses itself as service to others; only with compassion can you forgive. It is compassion and love that dissolves the ego and bring humility. Compassion is the fountainhead of all other virtues. Buddha embodied compassion and the Dalai Lama speaks so much on it. Jesus was the messenger of love. Krishna embodied divine love. The basis, the fabric, the essence of all spiritual–religious traditions is love and compassion. Love, with existence and consciousness, is the substratum of existence, if established in one; the other two come along like three legs of a stool. God created love equally in all humans, universally, unlike intellect, which He distributed differently. From an illiterate peasant to the President of a country, each one has the same love, even though the expressions may differ.

Compassion has also opened me to receiving from others, got me listening to others. When I'm so caught up within, it cuts people out, and I'm not so sensible and sensitive to others. It is compassion that has melted my own concepts and opinions. I listen to others more and accept others just the way they are, with a smile. However, acceptance is within, so it doesn't mean I accept negative people and not do anything. No! I am still dynamic in action. First, accept the fact that someone doing or saying something immoral or unethical and then so something about it. This is one of the points in the Art of Living course also.

Showing compassion to others should come with dispassion. Those who are sensitive tend to get entangled and drown themselves in someone else's problem. It is good to help someone, but also maintain a distance within, like a doctor who cares for a patient without becoming emotionally involved or miserable as well. At another level of understanding it is good to know that suffering comes from a person's own ignorance and past Karma. So while caring for others is one's Dharma, also remember that this is all a play of Karma.

The knowledge I practice is the knowledge I have gained. The rest is still in theory, which I'm still working on integrating. Knowledge in practice comprises virtues and values. Krishna lists twenty values in the thirteenth chapter of the Gita, and in the sixteenth chapter how these manifest as traits of a noble person. These are prerequisites to spiritual seeking. So you should live this knowledge as values—this will automatically make you spiritual. If values are like the beads, love and compassion together are the thread, and this necklace once woven is adorned by the Self.

In a world that is becoming so oriented toward technology and so busy, where life is getting so complex and values seem to be degenerating, let me, let us, revive this compassion. Compassion is simple, natural, and universal. It will lead to happiness.

9 AH...BLISS!

What is it that I really want in life? There are so many things that I want, or want to get rid of in life, why? Because I want to be happy. Through all pursuits it is really happiness we pursue. Isn't that what we're all looking for? There is a Whitney Houston song, "Greatest Love", with the line, "I found the greatest love of all inside of me!" It is the same with happiness. Happiness is our nature that's why we want to get back to it; sadness isn't our nature that's why we want to get rid of it. I often repose in my Self with this knowing and experience the source of bliss within.

Sometimes we seem so far from happiness, it is hard to imagine that it's our nature. So what is our true nature, negativity or something else? I read this today by Deepak Chopra, in answer to a question:

"You said you have found your true self. When the real self is established, it is not concerned or bothered with extraneous thoughts. All negativity is recognized as foreign to its true nature, so there is no trying to get rid of negative thoughts, they fade away on their own out of neglect. If you aren't attached to thoughts, then you disempower them—you unplug their energy and they stop."

I have been listening to a commentary on the Chandogya Upanishad. When I thought about writing on "happiness" a few months ago, the very next chapter in the Upanishad, coincidently, happened to be on happiness! This Upanishad has three chapters on the nature of consciousness. There are three primary characteristics of "Atman," or soul, as mentioned earlier, which are *"Sat"* (existence), *"Chit"* (consciousness), and *"Anand"* (bliss or happiness). In chapter three, verse twenty-three talks about where to find this happiness that we are seeking:

"Yo vai bhuma tat sukham, nalpe sukham asti, bhumaiva sukham, bhuma tveva vijijnasitavya iti, bhumanam, bagavah, vijijnasa iti."

Translation by Swami Krishnanada:

"Happiness is plenum, happiness is completeness, happiness is the totality, happiness is in the Absolute. The term *'Bhuma'* used in this Upanishad is a novel word of its own kind which cannot be easily translated. It has a pregnant significance within itself which implies absoluteness in quantity as well as in quality, an uncontaminated character, and permanency of every type, immortality, infinity and eternity. All these ideas are embedded in the very concept of what the Upanishad calls *'Bhuma.'* Well, we can translate it in no other way than to call it the Absolute Being. The Brahman of all the Upanishads is the same as the *Bhuma* mentioned here in this Chhandogya Upanishad. That alone is happiness."

And *"Tat Tvam Asi,"* I am That (happiness).

"Nalpe sukham asti" - the finite things do not contain happiness.

When I heard this, I fell in love with this word *"Bhuma."* The sound and the feeling when I said it gave me a sense of expansion. The experience of this fullness within was so real that having tasted that, the transient happiness from the world seemed like a shadow. It is a great asset to know that I am happiness that I don't have to depend on anything or anyone to be happy. Also, if I'm unhappy I have caused it, not someone else; it's all internal. Unhappiness can come from reacting to something, and reacting actually comes due to attachment or desires from my opinions, ideas, seeking perfection, or expecta-tions. Lack of compassion also causes reactions and unhappiness. All this is finally due to a lapse of wisdom. Wise people are naturally centered and in bliss all the time.

Like I'd mentioned, I thought of writing this chapter a few months ago when my life was hunky dory. Now, when I have actually started writing this chapter, I'm going through one of the most difficult and stressful times in my life. My father has just passed away; I have started a new job; I am worried about my mother; my husband just had surgery; we need to move homes, wind up my mom's home, and move her here; and I am anxious about it all working out.

So I'm writing a chapter on happiness at an "unhappy" time in my life!

My dad's passing has been a soul-searching experience because everything that I believe in is being tested, like "the soul is eternal" and "death is like changing clothes." It is also a test to see how I react to my father's passing. If I have the wisdom manifested within I will be unperturbed inside and still be in touch with my true nature, which is bliss. On the outside it has been stressful with so many things happening at the same time. I am so glad that I've invested in Yoga, Pranayama, Sudarshan Kriya, and meditation. They are a real savior in troubled times. But I'm still searching for that happiness.

So what do we mean by "happiness"? A lot of people associate the word with an emotional state that is usually connected with pleasure and comfort. But this is temporary, and happens when something "good" happens. There is nothing wrong with that happiness either, but usually it goes away—it's just a matter of time, and then we're looking for happiness again, chasing a mirage. So it is not this emotional elation we feel; absolute happiness can't be an emotion. We can buy a car, house, a vacation, and many other things that give us momentary happiness, but true happiness can't be bought at any cost.

Temporary happiness comes from fulfilled desires, thinking about me and mine, and eventually leaves us looking for permanent happiness. I see a lot of people who seem happy, but most people become unhappy at the loss of a family member, or loss of job/wealth/fame/power, or when diagnosed with a disease.

Most of us think of happiness as the opposite of unhappiness. Some say that unless you know deep sorrow you cannot know happiness. I am not talking about this pair of opposites, happiness/unhappiness. How can something that comes and goes be true happiness? No. I am referring to *bliss*, which is beyond the duality of happiness/unhappiness. I haven't counted how many times Sri Krishna mentions being free of 'Sukha-Dukha' (happiness/unhappiness) duality in the Bhagavad Gita. The nature of Atma (soul) is bliss. When we seek happiness, we are actually seeking the substratum of our existence—which is bliss.

The more we are established in this bliss that is permanent, unmoving, and unchanging, the less we will be brutally thrashed by the ups and downs of our emotions, battered by events and situations, and the less we will react to people.

Sri Sri Ravi Shankar says to be happy in the "now," in the present moment. He tells us not to postpone happiness. How often are we happy right now, without wanting something or waiting for something to happen in the future? How often is our happiness without conditions like "When this happens..." or "When I have this..."? How often are we in touch with that bliss inside, without a desire being fulfilled? True happiness is unconditional. Standing on top of a mountain, looking out at the vastness, or being in the open ocean and feeling that expanse, with arms open wide and the wind blowing on my face—ah! Bliss!

How often can we overcome challenges without becoming unhappy? We can feel sadness at the loss of our father, for example, but still stay unmoved inside, balanced, centered. This comes from being established in the Self and from the wisdom within I remain untouched. Are we in touch with a different quality of happiness in the core of our being, which is bliss? Or is it heavily covered with our mind, emotions, and existence? Rarely are we in touch with our Self. Like an ocean, there is turbulence on the surface, but as you dive deep into the ocean there is only calm, serenity, and silence.

The causes of misery are many. I know them, and they are stated in the scriptures as ignorance, ego, desires, aversions, and fear. The solutions for happiness are few, so let me seek them. Better than fighting the darkness is to light a candle. H. H. Dalai Lama says from "I want happiness," remove the "I" (ego), the "want" (desire) and you will be left with "happiness." The Vedas say that the true nature of the soul is "existence," "consciousness," and "bliss." So how am I to know that this is what I am? It is certainly a relief to know that I am not this angry, impatient, imperfect mass of flesh! But how can I be established in that bliss that supposedly I am? How am I to be happy? I gave it some thought and realized that I need to be dispassionate and compassionate—at the same time. This bliss is very close to the quality of unconditional compassion and devotion.

In the Bhagavad Gita, Sri Krishna mentions that one who has discipline and control over his senses and mind is a happy person. Sri Krishna also says that a disintegrated, undisciplined person cannot gain clarity of knowledge about Truth and therefore cannot contemplate or meditate. A person who can't meditate can't experience peace; he will remain restless. How can a restless person be happy?

In the sixth chapter of the Bhagavad Gita, Sri Krishna

75

discusses meditation and the happiness gained from it. That bliss is not of, and cannot be experienced by, the body, senses, or the mind; it is beyond that.

In *Vivekachoodamani*, Adi Shankaracharya says when people, situations, and things are conducive to our liking, we are happy. When they are not, we are unhappy. Therefore we become happy and unhappy because of our likes and dislikes and not any other reason. No external person or situation can make us happy or unhappy, meaning the source can't be outside. Our happiness or unhappiness depends upon how we look at the world. In different states of mind, the same person or thing can cause joy at one time and sorrow at another, based on our likes or dislikes. Happiness and unhappiness are created by our own minds because we give importance to some things and not to others.

Meditation brings me in touch with the core of my existence. There's a feeling of elevation. I don't know what it is, if it's just an experience or if it's for real, but it feels so good, deeply relaxing. I feel like I've come home and am happily resting; I can let go and relax. This ah! feeling you know…an expansion. I feel a peaceful bliss permeating and expanding from my heart. This presence is much larger…beyond my physical existence. I don't know exactly how to explain it. It's like a rose and its fragrance. This fragrance is the essence of the rose; it spreads much farther than the rose and cannot be seen. Being in touch with that essence, that fragrance transcends the rose, the physical body. And that fragrance is this bliss I'm talking about. That calm, sweet, tender, joyful fullness! In this fullness all desires have succumbed and there are no pestering thoughts. It's much easier to extract the fragrance of bliss from the rose within than to obtain bliss from the harsh world outside.

Swami Tejomayananda (Chinmaya Mission) has something very

intriguing in his "Tips for Happy Living." He says that when there is no integration between mind, intellect, and sense organs we can't be happy. Our intellect has a conviction for what is right, but our mind has its own temptations and cravings, and then the senses are extroverted and disintegrate the will further. Also, he says, there should be oneness in thoughts, words, and deeds. A lot of times we think one thing, say another, and do something completely different. How can we be happy with ourselves if these don't line up? There should be sweetness in our thoughts and this should flow to our words, and then spread sweetness through our actions— this will bring happiness to oneself and others. It starts from the source, the core of our being, the most subtle aspect, and it is all bliss.

How can bliss come from anything temporary? Yet all our desires are for temporary things, and unhappiness is also from transient events. Then happiness and unhappiness are temporary as well. Nothing that changes can be said to be absolute truth or real. The cause of desire is ignorance, the attachment to this physical existence. That's why I said this bliss has to be devoid of desires, which is dispassion, and dispassion is not dry or empty, it is full of compassion. Bliss can only be regained, rediscovered, uncovered from the realization of our true nature, which is eternal bliss. Let me take it for granted until I shed this ignorance. Let me meditate and get in touch with it again and again...

"The bliss the scriptures are talking about cannot be induced artificially because it is not related to the physical or the mental or even the intellectual plane. In fact, one cannot do anything to bring it about. One just prepares oneself and awaits its happening as a realization. It is not a 'state.' One becomes of the nature of bliss," said Sri Ananadamayi Ma.

The journey of life is to go from the head to the spiritual heart. Even though I earnestly seek liberation, let me take it for granted that I am a reflection of that free Self. The grand design is making everything happen. Like the cycle of sunrise and sunset, this creation is moving from creation towards dissolution, only to be created again. My current understanding of myself as being a limited being, a speck in the grand scheme of things is an incomplete understanding. I am the absolute-being, the Brahman, whose dream is this creation. I AM! Who knows if all this is true, and whether I will ever know. Let me work on being happy, internalize good virtues and values to be a good human being. Let me implement what I know and live from my heart. This life, people, this world, and all of creation is an amazing mystery. My mind and my perceptions create my reality. My mind goes from one understanding about life and the world to another; it keeps evolving and changing. It feels like we reject a previous understanding like a delusion and create a new delusionary view. The mind creates worlds within worlds, but when I transcend the mind, through meditation, I feel permanence. There is something that is permanent...On a few occasions in life I have seen this life as a dream.

10 THE PERFECTED ONE

As a river starts in the mountains, young and frisky, it's active—like the Karma Yoga phase. Then when it comes down to the plains it calms down in its middle age, like the Upasana phase (meditation, etc.). Finally, in its ripe old age it can understand wisdom, like the Jnan phase (knowledge). The final stage is the merging into the ocean: there is no separate river or its water—it's all one, like enlightenment. What is enlightenment? What is the nature of an enlightened person?

As Sri Sri Ravi Shankar puts it, the process of enlightenment is to go from something to nothing to everything. I know I am definitely not just a piece of flesh. Yes, it's part of me, and I function through it, but not just the body alone. I can't just be the breath—it can't exist on its own without the body and mind. The mind can be without the body, but something is making it function, which is the intellect. The intellect is coming from somewhere; something makes it shine. It's like the sun's glimmers on a bucket of water. I can still witness all these so I can be none of these. I do find it hard to go beyond the "I" reference point. That, too, has a source, and that unknown is called consciousness. This is not a thing, so it's nothing, but it is the existence principle itself, the source that makes this human system function. This existence is conscious—it's the conscious principle itself, so it's not intelligent but intelligence, not knowledgeable but knowledge itself. This existence-consciousness is not dull or void, but it is bliss itself. That is finally my true source then, existence–consciousness–bliss.

If it's my true source, then it's also for everyone else. Though each one of us has a different body, different thoughts, opinions, intellectual levels, and egos, it is the source manifesting in a variety of personalities. Like the white light that breaks up into an infinite number of colors. Essentially, I should be aware of this underlying oneness between me and others. Enlightened people always see the substratum, consciousness, which is both immediate and transcendental.

Objects also exist, so they, too, have to have the existence as source. If you trace the source of matter, you will see it will also end up in consciousness. We as a human race are at the brink of this great discovery in science. Also, from a creation standpoint, earth came from water, which condensed from fire balls. Fire came from gas and air. Air came from space and space came from consciousness. So then the basis of matter is also consciousness. No wonder enlightened beings see only consciousness in and through everything and everyone.

If the unseen substratum is consciousness, and there is no cause or source of this consciousness, that has to be the ultimate reality. If it is "real," it can't change. It is without form, it has no "separateness," therefore it undivided and without a second (*Advaita*). Since it's not an object it can't be perceived by the mind, and anyway, it's beyond the mind, so it can't be captured or comprehended. It is also beyond logic, so it has to be just "Being." I can't imagine the state of an enlightened person. They have a body, mind, intellect, and ego (in some measure) but the way these instruments function is from being established in consciousness rather than from the ego, like the rest of us. Ramana Maharishi wrote:

> "There is nothing wrong in seeing anything, this body or the world. The mistake lies in thinking you are the body. There is no harm in thinking the body is in you. The body, world, all must be in the Self; or rather nothing can exist apart from the Self, as no pictures can be seen without the screen on which the shadows can be cast."

If the enlightened person has no sense of separateness, they probably see everyone like a play of colors of light, or like waves in the ocean. Each wave has a name and form but is essentially still the ocean. There must be so much peace within. How can someone *be* existence–consciousness–bliss 24/7? Wow!

The state of mind of such an enlightened one is described by Sri Vidhyaranya Swami as:

> *"Even if the clouds of Maya (illusion of creation) pour down torrential rain as and when they please, it cannot touch or taint the space. Similarly, even if the mind pours down the waters of thought, the Self, the Consciousness never gets affected by them at all."*

So how does such a realized soul live and transact in the world while reveling in the glory of the Self all the time? It is from right thinking. When one functions from an expanded-infinite consciousness, one identifies with the whole. Always has the benefit of all in mind. This is the basis of all ethical and moral values.

In Situations

In all situations it is the body, mind, or ego that is interacting with the world. All experiences come in pairs of opposites: health and sickness, pleasure and pain, and so on. Praise and insult are interpreted by the intellect and affect our ego. The benefit of being enlightened is that in an enlightened state one still experiences everything at the body, mind, intellectual, and ego levels but remains unattached, unaffected, a witness to all, therefore never moving from that permanent state of expanded awareness, peace, and bliss. We, however, function from the ego, intellect, mind, or body level and keep getting thrashed up and down with the experience of the pair of opposites.

With Inert Objects

If that separateness is dropped, then everything is that one consciousness. Everything is a part of consciousness, everything is divine. Nothing is really outside of consciousness. Being that infinite consciousness, how can anyone have greed for objects? On the mental level, they will seem as solidified consciousness. They are already yours. However, on the transaction level, due importance has to be given to each one, used for the correct purpose to sustain oneself and serve others. One has to value money, house, car, gadgets, and the like because each one can use for a good purpose. The difference between a wise and an ignorant person is in the attitude toward things.

With Other Living Beings

An enlightened being looks at everyone as an expression of his own Self. Others' sorrows and happiness is his own. He treats everyone with equanimity and objectivity. Everyone belongs to him and he belongs to all. He is never affected by the negativity of others, and therefore never reacts, because he's established in the power of purity. He is absolutely at peace with the way people are and all their imperfections; he accepts them just the way they are. Don't we accept all the animals in the world just the way they are? You don't say that the snake should be like a deer. With this attitude he deals with people according to the need of the situation, time, and place. He has no expectations from others, therefore he never gets disappointed.

One who has dropped the mind and the ego is truly free of misery. He is not bound by the disturbances of the mind. Like the saint Kabir said, *"I am the space of Consciousness in which the aero plane of the mind is flying here and there. Where can the mind go? Can it go out of Consciousness? How can the space of Consciousness have distractions? Even the wanderings and restlessness of the mind is reveling in the Self alone."*

When I see the world, I see definite inert objects like the desk, car, etc. I absolutely see my body as separate from others and others as a completely different entity. No, I don't see consciousness running in and through everything. Yes, sometimes I see the same life energy in others as myself, but then I see their personalities as separate and super imposing on that something common I share with them at a deeper level.

I think when the muddy turbulent water has been completely purified, and gained unwavering calmness and clarity; the reflection of the true self is seen automatically without effort. It was always there but could not be seen.

Enlightenment is a mystery to me. It's supposed to be my nature even now, so, technically, I'm already enlightened but I just have not realized it yet. I would like to in this life. I have also been afraid of Samadhi and enlightenment for a long time. One day I had a revelation while brushing my teeth (strange but true!). I have had states of no-mind, where in meditation I have no thoughts; I blank out, like deep sleep. Then when I come back it feels like only a fraction of a second has passed, but it would have been several minutes or even an hour or more. When I do come back, I am in an expanded state of consciousness, in a witness state, in total bliss, like a crystal. It's hard to explain. Anyway, I was thinking about enlightenment, that perhaps you go into a deep Samadhi and you do come back, but you're different, you're pure existence–consciousness–bliss. Like Buddha. So enlightenment is similar to my small experience of this, but a permanent state. So I'm no longer scared of the unknown state of realization.

Everything in creation is cyclical. I live with the mental comfort that: (1) This creation itself is an illusion, like a dream. (2) Everything gets created, destroyed, and created again, so why get stuck? (3) Everything is just happening and is taken care of by design, so why worry? Just go with the flow.

What is amazing is that through our experiences we move from one mental illusion or delusion to the next. I have gained certain knowledge, had certain experiences, and these form certain ideas and concepts in my mind, which in turn affect my judgment, perception, ideas, beliefs, assumptions, decisions, interpretations, everything. All these form my mental world, which I live in, and believe to be reality. Each one of us lives in our own bubble of reality. Then, when I gain more knowledge, more experience —spiritual and practical—I build a new mental world for myself. I know people who have gained some spiritual knowledge and have had some spiritual experiences and they live in an illusion that they have gotten somewhere. That illusion is harder to get out than that of an ignorant person. Intriguing. I also hear and meet a lot of spiritual people and spiritual teachers, and in them I see things like ego, desires, anger, and so on. Amazingly, they don't see it in themselves. They are also in a state of delusion. I am also in some delusion and move from one illusionary world to the next. What is reality? What is "normal"? What is the truth?

What's better is to be a good human being, absorb virtues and values and live them every moment. Be aware of negativity and eliminate it using practices, awareness, and wisdom. Always be practical, skillful, and compassionate with everyone in the world. So I don't want to talk about knowledge nowadays, I want to live it. The knowledge I have really gained is that which I live and practice. The rest is just what I have studied like we study in school. I have seen people talk the highest knowledge and not live the basics. What's the point? It's useless. Better to live the basics and let the highest knowledge dawn naturally, like the ripening of a fruit.

Life goes on and my pursuit of truth and happiness continues. In the end, everything works out fine, it happened exactly as designed. This body will drop one day. Who knows if I have a soul that will move on to another world and then come back in another body. The world will keep turning through the eras to come. Who knows what will happen to this universe. Does it really matter? Smile...be happy!

11 DEAR SON

What do I leave behind after I'm gone? In a dusty, faded, ornate box they will find a letter to my son. Just kidding—it will be in electronic format online! The only people I have a right and a duty to be an adviser and a guide to are my children. Whatever I say to them, whether I scold them, or say no to them, is for their good, without being afraid of being disliked, because unconditional love is always about the other person. May this letter be something that will be with him whenever he needs me, even after I am no more…

Dear Raj,

Several years ago in a hospital room in Chicago you came into this world! You are the happiest child I've ever known. From the point of my pregnancy till today, your father and I only remember your smiling face; and whenever I think of you it makes me smile. You are always loving, sweet, pleasant, friendly with everyone, never any trouble, so grounded, centered, responsible, sensible, and amazingly wise for your age. I am so grateful to the divine that he gave me such a tender loving soul. Love you, my dearest one. You're a part of my soul!

In you I see very few shortcomings, if any, so I really have no advice for you. On the contrary there is so much I can learn from you. I have known you longer than anyone else; from the time you were in my womb. I know who you are, your essence, I know you to the core! You are such a wonderful, gentle, loving human being, with a beautiful heart. Remember this. In a lot of ways you are wiser than me, better in the ways of the world, and in dealing with people.

The next wave in our civilization and human evolution will be defined by your generation. I see in you a more evolved human being than our generation in terms of refinement, sensitivity, and subtleness. I hope and pray that the next generation will take with it the baton of the ancient knowledge that has been passed down thousands of years through our lineage. As the world becomes more mechanical it's important to remember and be in touch with the spirit within, it's that which makes us human. Inert objects simply exist, animals have consciousness, but only humans can experience that state of Bliss!

If you do go into a scientific profession, I hope that you will be open minded about incorporating the ancient wisdom on the mind, body, and spirit. Science is not the ultimate truth, as it's always changing. It can, to some degree, explain the tangible world in a logical way. However as only 4% of the universe is matter, the rest 96% is dark matter and energy unknown to current science, so there's a lot we don't know and will never know. Beyond the realm of measured reality, is an unbound ultimate reality that is our essence, and this reality is both immanent as well as transcendental. You may have new perspectives and revelations on existence, consciousness, and the human mind. Your generation will reveal the truth in a different light, and the new *Rishis* (spiritual seers) will be born.

Though scientific you have very good people skills. What impresses me is that you can read people so well and so quickly! Such amazing qualities you have, dear one. Inside you is an eternal light, a living pulsating consciousness, gentle love, and soothing grace. Bask in its abundance. Be grateful to the divine who placed these great virtues in you, and gave you so many achievements.

What is our greatest quality? It is love. Let us always take love for granted, in others, and in you. Know that your parents love you unconditionally. Know that you are lovable, and that you are so loving! The only thing real is love. Ice melts to become water again, vapor condenses back to water, water always returns to its natural state, so too we always return to our compassionate and happy self, it's our natural state! How uncomfortable we feel with feelings of dislike, hatred, unhappiness. Then how can that be our nature? Our default nature is made up of love. Nature will make you flow back to your Self.

Be yourself. All philosophies finally give you this message. We tend to get tangled in so much deep thinking that we lose the perfection of the present moment. And no matter how much the mind fabricates, intellectualizes, and convinces, remember you are not the mind! The mind is like mist, the warmth of the heart is like the sun, when it dawns the mist disappears, the veil lifts, and you see your true self. So we should live from our heart; the heart is not complicated like the mind. Our mind is very complex and puts so many labels on ourselves and others. The whole journey of a human is to go from the head to the (spiritual) heart.

That inner core, the heart, the soul, is the source of our existence. The moment, by any of the methods, you affect subsidence or merger of the mind into its source, the divine energy rushes forth, spouting as from a spring within you. There is no question that you love yourself and others, we are love, and always struggling to go back to feeling that way. I have seen you living only from the state of compassion. I can't remember a time when you have not been loving, caring, and compassionate. Therefore; I have very rarely seen angry in you, your words have never hurt anyone, there's so much sweetness in your speech. You have had the most peaceful adolescence!

Our effort should be to become effortless existence, being simple and natural. Happiness comes from being simple and natural, and my dear son, you exemplify that to us. When we feel the love and happiness within, we don't need to look for it anywhere else. What do happy loving people do? They make others happy! In fact when unhappy if we pray to God with love, or serve others more miserable than us, we actually feel better.

Whatever we focus on is what grows. The natural tendency of the mind to run into the gullies of negative thought patterns. If we could only observe the mind, that very moment we detach from it. All we need to consciously shift our attention from negative thoughts to things we want to expand in life. Perceive yourself as spirit; listen to the voice of your heart, your soul. Just doing compassion meditation, meditating on the words, "Peace, Love, Compassion, Bliss," brings forth the experience of them. It triggers related centers in the brain, rewires our brain, and therefore changes the pattern of our thoughts. Our nature state is bliss. Our pure essence is love. Realize your magnificence! We need to let go now all the ideas and definitions we have about ourselves. We need to start life afresh every moment. That way your mind is free. You have to let go of all the thoughts, opinions and beliefs that don't serve our highest purpose, to realize that we are existence-consciousness-bliss.

I was just pondering on the question of what is considered "normal," and what is considered "good" or "right"? I think that it depends on the outcome. When we do something that is beneficial to us in the *long term* (not short term) it is "good" for us. So we should drop the urge to act on thoughts that don't serve us. If we do impulsively act on "bad" thoughts and emotions then what? For example, I get angry, or feel guilt, and then what will that do? What good is that? It doesn't serve any purpose. It will only be destructive. If only we realized up front that there's no point in actualizing negative desires.

What is "right"? I think whenever something is NOT illegal, immoral, unhealthy, or unsafe it is "right" for us, and our civilized humanity. These are the boundaries within which we consider ourselves as "normal".

It's just about compassion, dear one. It is compassion that makes us human. Otherwise we are just a piece of flesh with an ego. These are the simple values to live by, no need for complicated philosophies. All other virtues flow from compassion. The closer a person is to you, the more negativity you will see in them. One needs to love people not because of what they are but despite of what they are. Take it for granted that you are compassionate, that you *are* compassion.

Compassion starts with you. Be kind to yourself. Be full with love and respect for the divine form that you are. Others can love you only as much as you love yourself. Love yourself unconditionally.

Only compassion evaporates the ego in all its forms. Only love dispels all delusions, illusions, and impressions of the mind. It is love that drops you from the head to the heart, to the seat of the soul.

Remember a compassionate heart is not weak. The power of compassion can withstand any up or down. Its brilliance is that of a thousand suns, and darkness dare not come near it. Be strong yet sensitive, like a powerful yet compassionate king who will serve his people but will also raise arms to defend his kingdom, and himself. In fact, only love can bring true lasting strength, because it is the only thing that is without conflict or ego. Have that unwavering love within. It is a conviction of the self.

While feeling free inside, and knowing that you *are* love, balance it equally when engaging outside. For the outside you need two main things, strength/energy/dynamism, and skill in dealing with people and situations. So one needs to be practical, and excel in the world also. It's absolutely necessary to have equal balance inside and outside, between the ideal and real, between theoretical and practical, between knowledge and action.

For action one needs energy. For a positive and healthy mind, raise the level of energy. Do some physical exercises also in addition to Pranayamas and meditation. You eat healthy food already, so that is another source of energy. The thoughts always have a tendency to flow into the deeply ingrained pathways of degenerative tendencies. Observe this. Strength of mind is developed using your will, sharp intellect, and all of the above. Our evolution is in moving from a mind leading us into unwanted habits to a life in which wisdom and righteousness conducts.

In life nothing will be ten out of ten; at most they will be eight out of ten. You decide which eight are important to you.
Remember give your 100 percent and never even think about the result, let alone being driven by the outcome of your efforts. Your expectations for the results will, in fact, suffocate your efforts, and give you a lot of stress. You will never regret any loss if you have given it your all, but will regret if you have not. Haven't you experienced this? Then why suffer?

Always be the way you are today, strong and self-confident. Don't hang on to what others think about you, drop them and move on. Never take anyone's negativity seriously; close the shutters when it comes your way, because their negativity will go away and it will on stay in you. So it's better you shun others' negativity with strength and dispassion. If they dislike you it's their *Karma*, how you respond is yours.

Be wise about the company you seek. Without intimidation, make friends with and be in the company of the strong, wise, successful, and conventional people. They will take you upward. The company you keep has a huge influence on you.

Bow down, do *Pranaam* (ablutions), to *Bhagawan* (God) every day. If you can have a puja place (shrine) where you can have a few sacred moments, close your eyes and pray. Then touch the feet of the Lord, bowing the head. This brings a tremendous amount of humility, reverence, gratitude, devotion, and kindles that divinity within us. When love is directed to the divine it will be ever pure and free of pain. It is the only love worth living for. Emotional love is a mirage; do not chase it, it will lead you astray and leave you thirsty and weak. In relationships always have compassion without attachment, even with your lady love, your children, and your parents.

Our scriptures say: worship your mother as God, worship your father as God, worship your Guru as God, and worship your guest as God. If you have this attitude, willingly, you will receive tremendous amounts of love and blessings in your life always. I am so glad that you are learning the Bhagavad Gita - it is the most comprehensive guidance on living, and knowledge on creation and consciousness.

So much wisdom! Oh, my God! You must be overwhelmed reading it! Take it lightly and just have fun this life-time. We think we have to do this and that, but should we be so serious about life and try to control it? One day when Papa and I were walking, we saw a father pushing his son's toy bike from behind, the boy was busy pedaling but the pedals were not connected to the wheels! Just like that we are busy pedaling through life, but really it's God pushing our bike from behind. He is taking us through this "World's Carnival," and though we keep pedaling, we should just smile and enjoy!

Always remember one thing: your parents love you no matter

what. It doesn't matter sometimes we scold you, but you must confide in us. We are the only ones in the world who truly care about what's best for you. Know that you can take us for granted, you can be with us, this will always be your home, no matter how far you may go in the world or how long you are away. Family is always family; others come and go. I am always there for you, my dearest one!

With love,
Mama

Om Tat Sat

DEDICATION

भगवत परसादात सत गुरु परसादो हृदि पुष्प त्वत पाद भक्तमि समर्पयामो गुरु-रवि शंकराय क्रपया वधिहि शिरिसा नमामि

Bhagavat Prasādāt Sat Guru Prasādo Hridi-Pushpa Tvat-Pāda-Bhaktim Samarpayāmo Guru Ravi Shankarāya Kripayā Videhi Shirisā Namāmi

Translation:
By the grace of Sri Krishna I have received the benediction of a Sat Guru. I offer the flowers of my heart with devotion at the feet of my Guru Ravi Shankara. Please bless me, I bow down to you.

ABOUT THE AUTHOR

Vinita was born in Kanpur, India. She has lived in and traveled to several cities around the world. Her family lived in Zambia (Africa) for many years. She went to boarding school at St. Mary's, Nainital, India and then college in the US. Although her day time job is in the IT industry, her passions are comparative religions, quantum physics, spirituality, and well-being. She has been learning these for the last 25 years. She conducts workshops on yoga, meditation, and spirituality. Vinita is also enthusiastic about volunteering and has been involved in several service projects for non-profit organizations. She lives in the Silicon Valley with her husband and two sons.

MANTRA
BOOKS

We publish books on Eastern religions and philosophies.
Books that aim to inform and explore. This list also publishes
books on Advaita - nonduality. ("You see, in the final analysis,
there are not two things; there is only nonduality.
That is the truth; that is Advaita."
quoted by Dennis Waite).